CORPORATE SOCIAL RESPONSIBILITY, GOVERNANCE AND CORPORATE REPUTATION

CORPORATE SOCIAL RESPONSIBILITY, GOVERNANCE AND CORPORATE REPUTATION

Petter Gottschalk
Norwegian School of Management, Norway

World Scientific

NEW JERSEY · LONDON · SINGAPORE · BEIJING · SHANGHAI · HONG KONG · TAIPEI · CHENNAI

Published by

World Scientific Publishing Co. Pte. Ltd.

5 Toh Tuck Link, Singapore 596224

USA office: 27 Warren Street, Suite 401-402, Hackensack, NJ 07601

UK office: 57 Shelton Street, Covent Garden, London WC2H 9HE

Library of Congress Cataloging-in-Publication Data
Gottschalk, Petter, 1950–
    Corporate social responsibility, governance and corporate reputation / by Petter Gottschalk.
    p. cm.
    Includes bibliographical references and index.
    ISBN-13: 978-981-4335-17-1
    ISBN-10: 981-4335-17-7
    1. Corporations--Corrupt practices. 2. White collar crimes. 3. Social responsibility of business.
4. Corporate governance. 5. Corporations--Public relations. I. Title.
    HV6768.G6848 2011
    658.4'7--dc22

                        2011001504

British Library Cataloguing-in-Publication Data
A catalogue record for this book is available from the British Library.

Typeset by Stallion Press
Email: enquiries@stallionpress.com

Printed in Singapore.

Preface

Corporate social responsibility, corporate governance and corporate reputation are important issues for business survival and success. Companies all over the world have implemented ethical guidelines, governance structures and routines for self-regulation and self-reporting. These approaches are necessary, but not always sufficient.

When companies are hit by white-collar crime, governance structures tend to collapse. This illustrates the formal rather the real contents of procedures implemented. Like many auditing cases associated with fraud, governance cases illustrate formal procedures rather than real prevention and control. Too often, responsibility and governance are issues found in the annual report but not in everyday business operations.

White-collar crime can be understood using the metaphors of "rotten apple", "rotten apple barrel" or "rotten apple garden". The individual approach is based on the rotten apple theory, where one person needs to be removed and prosecuted. The group approach is based on the rotten apple barrel theory, where a department needs to be removed or replaced. The organization approach is based on the rotten apple garden theory, where the system is such that the whole organization has a criminal structure in its business activities.

Depending on whether white-collar crime represents a rotten apple, barrel or garden, approaches to governance and the consequences for reputation will be very different indeed. That is what this book is about. I hope you learn from it.

Oslo, Norway
17 August 2010
Petter Gottschalk

Contents

Preface   v

Introduction   1

1. White-Collar Crime   3

White-Collar Crime Defined 4
White-Collar Crime Categories 9
Variety of White-Collar Crime 14
Theories of White-Collar Crime 19
Detection of White-Collar Crime 20

2. Corporate Reputation   27

Corporate Reputation Defined 27
Resource-Based Theory 29
Determinants of Corporate Reputation 31
Effects of Corporate Reputation 32
Theories of Corporate Reputation 33
Measurement of Corporate Reputation 34
Rebuilding Corporate Reputation 35
Social Responsibility and Corporate Reputation 36
Corporate Governance Ratings 37

3. Reputation Damage and Repair   39

Reputation Survey Design 39
Reputation Survey Results 41
Contingent Perspectives 42

Crime Determinants of Reputation   43
Reputation Effects from Crime   45
Ethics in Repair and Prevention   47
Investigating or Reporting   49
Sequence of Actions   51

4.   Internal Investigations   **53**

Corporate Investigation   53
Investigation Approaches   54
Investigator Performance   58
Investigator as Detective   60

5.   Corporate Compliance   **63**

Compliance Officer   64
Compliance Plan   65
Compliance Leadership   67
Self Regulation   68
Whistle Blowing   70
Compliance Levels   76

6.   Corporate Governance   **79**

Financial Statements   79
Governance Systems   80
Executive Roles at Risk   82
Governance Principles   86
Leader Types at Risk   88
Self-Regulation Governance   90
Influencing and Controlling   93
Responsible Business   94
Limits to Responsibility   95

7. **Stages of Corporate Responsibility**   97

Theory Building in Management Research   97
Stage Modeling in Management Research   99
Theory Building for Stage Models 101
Modeling Process for Stage Models 104
Corporate Social Responsibility 105
Frontiers of Corporate Responsibility 106
Internal Change Management 109
Stages of Corporate Social Responsibility 112

8. **Forensic Accounting**   117

Investigative Accounting 118
Cases of Forensic Audit 121
Deception Detection 122
Analytical Procedures 124
Suspicious Transactions 125
Money Laundering 126
Transaction Criteria 129
Information Processing 131

9. **Knowledge Management**   135

Knowledge Organization 135
Business Intelligence 141
Stages of Growth 145
Knowledge Resources 149
Core Competence 153
Entrepreneurship Capabilities 156
A Case of Dynamic Capabilities 158
Knowledge Driven Innovation 160

10.   Intelligence Strategy   **163**

Strategy Characteristics   163
Information Sources   165
Knowledge Categories   171
Value Shop Configuration   176

Conclusion   **181**

References   **183**

Index   **197**

Introduction

Corporate reputation is a global and general, temporally stable, evaluative judgment about a corporation that is shared by multiple stakeholders (Highhouse *et al.*, 2009). It is a long-term intangible corporate asset or liability that is important for organizational competitiveness (Friedman, 2009). It is a perceptual representation of a company's past actions and future prospects that describe the company's overall appeal to all its key constituents when compared to its rivals. Corporate reputation represents what is actually known by both internal and external stakeholders (Walker, 2010). Corporate reputation is the collective judgment of a corporation (Einwiller *et al.*, 2010). Reputation is a combination of reality such as economic and social performance and perception such as performance perceived by key stakeholders (Hemphill, 2006).

Corporate reputation is an important asset or liability bestowed upon a corporation by its stakeholders (Love and Kraatz, 2009). For example, if the stakeholders perceive a corporation to be corrupt or involved in other forms of white-collar crime, then corporate reputation is likely to be a liability rather than an asset. Awareness of the link between corporate reputation and white-collar crime has risen substantially in the business world after the joint collapse of Enron and Arthur Andersen. As a consequence, companies have become more sensitive to the value of their reputation. Corporate audiences, including institutional and individual investors, customers and suppliers, public authorities and competitors, evaluate the reputation of firms when making choices and other decisions (Linthicum *et al.*, 2010).

Classical examples of white-collar crime include business organizations such as Enron, Arthur Andersen, Siemens, WorldCom, and Royal Bank of Scotland. These examples are known throughout the world. But just as many, or even more examples are known locally in different countries. For example, in the five-million people country of Norway, a number of white-collar scandals have emerged in the last decade, such as Sponsor Service, PEAB and Finance Credit.

White-collar crime is financial crime with certain characteristics. It is a broad concept that covers illegal behavior that takes advantage of positions of professional authority and power (Kempa, 2010). White-collar crime can both benefit and harm business enterprises by being either an offender or a victim of crime. White-collar crime occurs in all kinds of organizations (Ventura and Daniel, 2010).

Links between white-collar crime and corporate reputation are explored in this book. Damage to corporate reputation caused by white-collar crime is discussed, and different approaches to reputation repair are presented. Other relevant topics such as internal investigations, corporate compliance, corporate governance, forensic accounting and detection of suspicious transactions are discussed. The book concludes by emphasizing the need for knowledge management to combat white-collar crime and to build corporate reputation.

Chapter 1

White-Collar Crime

The most economically disadvantaged members of society are not the only ones committing crime. Members of the privileged socioeconomic classes are also engaged in criminal behavior. The types of crime may differ from those of the lower classes, such as lawyers helping criminal clients launder their money, executives bribing public officials to achieve public contracts, or accountants manipulating balance sheets to avoid taxes. Another important difference between the two types of offenders is that the elite criminal is much less likely to be apprehended or punished due to his or her social status (Brightman, 2009).

The term white-collar crime expresses different concepts depending on perspective and context. In this book, white-collar crime is defined as financial crime committed by white-collar criminals. Thus, the definition includes characteristics of the crime as well as the criminal. Financial crime generally describes a variety of crimes against property, involving the unlawful conversion of property belonging to another for one's own personal use and benefit, more often than not involving fraud but also bribery, corruption, money laundering, embezzlement, insider trading, tax violations, cyber attacks and the like (Henning, 2009). Criminal gain for personal benefit seems to be one of the core characteristics of financial crime.

White-collar crime such as fraud, theft and corruption occur within companies (Acquaah-Gaisie, 2000; Toner, 2009). Company boards and top management are responsible for preventing such crime (Aldama *et al.*, 2009; Baer, 2008) as well as avoiding becoming involved themselves.

White-Collar Crime Defined

White-collar crime is a broad concept that covers illegal behavior that takes advantage of positions of professional authority and power — or simply the opportunity structures available within business — for personal or corporate gain. Crime such as corruption, embezzlement, fraud, insider trading, account misrepresentation and tax evasion add up to a significant criminal domain (Kempa, 2010). White-collar crime can both benefit and harm business enterprises as offender or victim respectively.

White-collar crime occurs in all kinds of organizations. As a prominent moral authority in our society, church organizations are probably the last places that people should expect to find crime such as corruption and embezzlement. The treasurer or church's business administrator is expected to handle the church's money with the highest moral and ethical standards. However, church executives steal from their own churches (Ventura and Daniel, 2010).

In the US, religious organizations receive close to one hundred billion dollars in charitable giving each year. Nearly two out of three households contribute to religious organizations, and three out of every four dollars contributed to charity went to religious centers. It is estimated that fifteen percent of all churches are at one time or another victimized by occupational fraud and organizational fraud (Ventura and Daniel, 2010).

One of the most influential criminologists seventy years ago was sociologist Edwin Sutherland. In his monograph on white-collar crime, he defined it as crime committed by persons of respectability and high social status in the course of their occupations. While many of the famous white-collar crime cases in the USA (e.g., Enron, Maddock, Siemens) were committed by individuals that fit this definition, others were perpetrated by regular white-collar workers such as bookkeepers and stock traders (Brody and Luo, 2009).

Edwin Sutherland introduced the concept of "white-collar" crime in 1939. According to Brightman (2009), Sutherland's theory was controversial, particularly since many of the academicians in the audience perceived themselves to be members of the upper echelons of American society. Despite his critics, Sutherland's theory of white-collar criminality served as the catalyst for an area of research that continues today. In particular, differential association theory proposes that a person associating with individuals who have deviant or unlawful mores, values, and norms learns criminal behavior. Certain characteristics play a key role in placing individuals in a position to behave unlawfully, including the proposition that criminal behavior is learned through interaction with other persons in the upper echelon, as well as interaction occurring in small intimate groups (Hansen, 2009).

Sutherland was a proponent of symbolic interactions perspectives and believed that criminal behavior was learned from interpersonal interaction with others. White-collar crime, therefore, overlaps with corporate crime because of the opportunity for fraud, corruption, embezzlement, insider trading and other illegal actions. Many denote the invention of Sutherland's idiom to the explosion of U.S. businesses in the years following the Great Depression. Sutherland noted at that time that less than two percent of the persons committed to prisons in a year belonged to the upper class.

In contrast to Sutherland, Brightman (2009) differs slightly regarding the definition of white-collar crime. While societal status may still determine access to wealth and property, he argues that the term white-collar crime should be broader in scope and include virtually any non-violent act committed for financial gain, regardless of one's social status. For example, access to technology, such as personal computers and the Internet, now allows individuals from all social classes to buy and sell stocks or engage in similar activities that were once the bastion of the financial elite.

In Sutherland's definition of white-collar crime, a white-collar criminal is a person of respectability and high social status who commits crime in the course of his occupation. This excludes many crimes of the upper class, as most of their cases of murder, adultery, and intoxication are not customarily a part of their procedures (Benson and Simpson, 2009). It also excludes lower class criminals who commit financial crime, as pointed out by Brightman (2009).

What Sutherland meant by respectable and high social status individuals is not quite clear, but in today's business world we can assume he meant to refer to business managers and executives. They are for the most part, individuals with power and influence that is associated with respectability and high social status. Part of the standard view of white-collar offenders is that they are mainstream, law-abiding individuals. They are assumed to be irregular offenders, not people who engage in crime on a regular basis (Benson and Simpson, 2009: 39):

> Unlike the run-of-the-mill common street criminal who usually has had repeated contacts with the criminal justice system, white-collar offenders are thought not to have prior criminal records.

When white-collar criminals appear before their sentencing judges, they can correctly claim to be first-time offenders. They are wealthy, highly educated, and socially connected. They are elite individuals, according to the description and attitudes of white-collar criminals as suggested by Sutherland.

Therefore, very few white-collar criminals are put on trial and even fewer upper class criminals are sentenced to imprisonment. This is in contrast to most financial crime sentences, where financial criminals appear in the justice system without being wealthy, highly educated, or socially connected.

White-collar criminals are not entrenched in criminal lifestyles like common street criminals. They belong to the elite in society, and they are typically individuals employed by and in legitimate organizations. According to Hansen (2009), individuals or groups commit occupational or elite crime for their own purposes or enrichment, rather than for the enrichment of the organization on a whole, in spite of supposed corporate loyalty.

Brody and Kiehl (2010) disagree with the view that white-collar criminals are not entrenched in criminal lifestyles including the use of violence. They use the term red-collar crime rather than white-collar crime to indicate that murder and other blood-related actions are carried out by white-collar criminals as well. They argue that white-collar criminals do display violent tendencies as well and, contrary to popular belief, can become dangerous individuals.

Bookman (2008) regards Sutherland's definition as too restrictive and suggests that white-collar crime is an illegal act committed by nonphysical means and by concealment or guile, to obtain money or property, to avoid payment or loss of money or property, or to obtain business or personal advantage. Furthermore, scholars have attempted to separate white-collar crime into two types: occupational and corporate. Occupational crime is committed largely by individuals or small groups in connection with their jobs. It includes embezzling from an employer, theft of merchandise, income tax evasion, manipulation of sales, fraud, and violations in the sale of securities. Corporate crime, on the other hand, is enacted by collectivities or aggregates of discrete individuals.

Pickett and Pickett (2002) use the terms "financial crime", "white-collar crime", and "fraud" interchangeably. They define white-collar crime as the use of deception for illegal gain, normally involving breach of trust and some concealment of the true nature of the activities. White-collar crime is often defined as crime against property, involving the unlawful conversion of property belonging to another for one's own personal use and benefit. Financial crime is profit-driven crime to gain access to and control over property that belonged to someone else.

Bucy *et al.* (2008) argue that white-collar crime refers to non-violent, business-related violations of state and/or federal criminal statues, and they make a distinction between "leaders" and "followers" in white-collar crime.

White-collar crime can be defined in terms of the offense, the offender or both. If white-collar crime is defined in terms of the offense, it means crime against property for personal or organizational gain. It is a property crime committed by non-physical means and by concealment or deception (Benson and Simpson, 2009). If white-collar crime is defined in terms of the offender, it means crime committed by upper class members of society for personal or organizational gain. Offenders are wealthy, highly educated, and socially connected individuals, and they are typically employed by and in legitimate organizations (Hansen, 2009).

If white-collar crime is defined in terms of both perspectives, it has the following characteristics:

➤ White-collar crime is crime against property for personal or organizational gain, which is committed by non-physical means and by concealment or deception. It is deceitful, it is intentional, it breaches trust, and it involves losses. White-collar crime is a type of offense involving property, economy and/or environment. It is characterized by deceit, concealment, or violation of trust, and it is not dependent upon the application or threat of physical force or violence.

➤ White-collar criminals are individuals who are wealthy, highly educated, and socially connected, and they are typically employed by and in legitimate organizations. They are persons of respectability and high social status who commit crime in the course of their occupations. White-collar crime is characterized by the type of offender, e.g., by social class or high socio-economic status, the occupation of positions of trust, profession, or academic qualification. Motivations for criminal behavior include greed or fear of loss of face if economic difficulties become obvious.

➢ In addition to type of offense and type of offender, white-collar crime can be characterized by the organizational culture. For example, the organizational culture can be such that corporate executives find it natural to commit criminal acts to benefit their company by overcharging or price fixing with competitors. Organizational culture is the set of values shared by organizational members. These values may include acceptance of criminal acts that benefit the organization and/or individuals in the organization.

In this book, we apply this definition of white-collar crime, where both characteristics of offense and offender identify the crime. Therefore, white-collar crime is only a subset of financial crime in our perspective: White-collar crime is the violation of the law by one holding a position of respect and authority in the community who uses his or her legitimate occupation to commit financial crime (Eicher, 2009). White-collar crime contains several clear components (Pickett and Pickett, 2002): It is deceitful, it is intentional, it breaches trust, it involves losses, it may be concealed, and there may be an appearance of outward respectability.

White-Collar Crime Categories

White-collar crime can be classified into categories as illustrated in Figure 1. There are two dimensions in the table. First, a distinction is made between leader and follower. This distinction is supported by Bucy et al. (2008), who found that motives for leaders are different from follower motives. Compared to the view that leaders engage in white-collar crime because of greed, followers are non-assertive, weak people who trail behind someone else, even into criminal schemes. Followers may be convinced of the rightness of their cause, and they believe that no harm can come to them because they are following a leader whom they trust or fear. Followers tend to be naive and unaware of what is really happening, or they are simply

Actor \ Role	Leader	Follower
Occupational	Occupational crime as leader	Occupational crime as follower
Corporate	Corporate crime as leader	Corporate crime as follower

Figure 1.   Categories of White-Collar Crime Depending on Role and Actor.

taken in by the personal charisma of the leader and are intensely loyal to that person.

Next, a distinction is made between occupational crime and corporate crime in Figure 1. It is largely individuals or small groups in connection with their jobs who commit occupational crime. It includes embezzling from an employer, theft of merchandise, income tax evasion, manipulation of sales, fraud, and violations in the sale of securities (Bookman, 2008). Occupational crime is sometimes labeled "elite crime". Hansen (2009) argues that the problem with occupational crime is that it is committed within the confines of positions of trust and in organizations, which prohibits surveillance and accountability. Heath (2008) found that the bigger and more severe occupational crimes tend to be committed by individuals who are further up the chain of command in a firm.

Corporate crime, on the other hand, is enacted by collectivities or aggregates of discrete individuals. If a corporate official violates the law in acting for the corporation, it is considered a corporate crime as well. But if he or she gains personal benefit in the commission of a crime against the corporation, it is occupational crime. A corporation cannot be jailed, and therefore, the majority of penalties to control individual violators are not available for corporations and corporate crime (Bookman, 2008).

In legal terms, a corporation is an unnatural person (Robson, 2010: 109):

> Corporate personality functions between an insentient, inanimate object and a direct manifestation of the acts and intentions of its managers. Nowhere is this duality more problematic than in the application of traditional concepts of criminal law to business organizations. The question of whether business organizations can be criminally liable — and if so, the parameters of such liability — has long been the subject of scholarly debate. Whatever the merits of such debate, however, pragmatic considerations have led courts and legislatures to expand the panoply of corporate crime in order to deter conduct ranging from reprehensible, to undesirable, to merely annoying. In the context of organizational behavior, criminal law is the ultimate deterrent.

Corporations become victims of crime when they suffer a loss as a result of an offense committed by a third party, including employees and managers. Corporations become perpetrators of crime when managers or employees commit financial crime within the context of a legal organization. According to Garoupa (2007), corporations can more easily corrupt enforcers, regulators and judges, as compared to individuals. Corporations are better organized, are wealthier and benefit from economies of scale in corruption. Corporations are better placed to manipulate politicians and the media. By making use of large grants, generous campaign contributions and influential lobbying organizations, they may push law changes and legal reforms that benefit their illegal activities.

Occupational crime is typically motivated by greed, where white-collar criminals seek to enrich themselves personally. Similarly, firms engage in corporate crime to improve their financial performance. Employees break the law in ways that enhance the profits of the firm, but which may generate very little or no personal benefit for themselves when committing corporate crime (Heath, 2008: 600):

> There is an important difference, for instance, between the crimes committed at Enron by Andrew Fastow, who secretly enriched himself at the expense of the firm, and those committed by Kenneth

Lay and Jeffrey Skilling, who for the most part acted in ways that enriched the firm, and themselves only indirectly (via high stock price).

While legal corporations may commit business crime, illegal organizations are in the business of committing crime. Garoupa (2007) emphasized the following differences between organized crime and business crime: (i) organized crime is carried out by illegal firms (with no legal status), the criminal market being their primary market and legitimate markets, secondary markets, (ii) corporate crime is carried out by legal firms (with legal status), the legitimate market being their primary market and the criminal market their secondary market. Whereas organized crime exists to capitalize on criminal rents and illegal activities, corporations do not exist to violate the law. Organized crime gets into legitimate markets in order to improve its standing on the criminal market, while corporations violate the law so as to improve their standing on legitimate markets.

Criminal opportunities are now recognized as an important cause of all crime. Without an opportunity, there cannot be a crime. Opportunities are important causes of white-collar crime, where the opportunity structures may be different from those of other kinds of crime. These differences create special difficulties for control, but they also provide new openings for control (Benson and Simpson, 2009).

While occupational crime is associated with bad apples, corporate crime is associated with systems failure. Bad apples theory represents an individualistic approach in criminology, while systems failure theory represents a business approach in criminology (Heath, 2008: 601):

If the individualistic approach were correct, then one would expect to find a fairly random distribution of white collar crime throughout various sectors of the economy, depending upon where individuals suffering from poor character or excess greed wound up working. Yet, what one finds instead are very high concentrations of criminal activity in particular sectors of the economy. Furthermore, these pockets of crime often persist quite stubbornly over time, despite a complete changeover in the personnel involved.

It is certainly an interesting issue whether to view white-collar misconduct and crime as acts of individuals perceived as "rotten apples" or as an indication of systems failure in the company, the industry or the society as a whole. The perspective of occupational crime is favoring the individualistic model of deviance, which is a human failure model of misconduct and crime. This rotten apple view of white-collar crime is a comfortable perspective to adopt for business organizations as it allows them to look no further than suspect individuals. It is only when other forms of group (O'Connor, 2005) and/or systemic (Punch, 2003) corruption and other kinds of crime erupt upon a business enterprise that a more critical look is taken of white-collar criminality. Furthermore, when serious misconduct occurs and is repeated, there seems to be a tendency to consider crime as a result of bad practice, lack of resources or mismanagement, rather than acts of criminals.

The "rotten apple" metaphor has been extended to include the group-level view of cultural deviance in organizations with a "rotten barrel" metaphor (O'Connor, 2005). Furthermore, Punch (2003) has pushed the notion of "rotten orchards" to highlight deviance at the systemic level. Punch (2003:172) notes, "the metaphor of 'rotten orchards' indicate[s] that it is sometimes not the apple, or even the barrel, that is rotten but the *system* (or significant parts of the system)".

Including rotten apple and rotten barrel concepts in Figure 2 expands Figure 1.

White-collar crime involves some form of social deviance and represents a breakdown in social order. According to Heath (2008), white-collar criminals tend to apply techniques of neutralization

Actor / Role		Leader	Follower
Occupational	Rotten apple	Occupational apple leader	Occupational apple follower
	Rotten barrel	Occupational barrel leader	Occupational barrel follower
Corporate	Rotten apple	Corporate apple leader	Corporate apple follower
	Rotten barrel	Corporate barrel leader	Corporate barrel follower

Figure 2. Categories of White-Collar Crime Depending on Role, Actor and Level.

used by offenders to deny the criminality of their actions. Examples of neutralization techniques are (1) denial of responsibility, (2) denial of injury, (3) denial of the victim, (4) condemnation of the condemners, (5) appeal to higher loyalties, (6) everyone else is doing it, and (7) claim to entitlement. The offender may claim an entitlement to act as he did, either because he was subject to a moral obligation, or because of some misdeed perpetrated by the victim. These excuses are applied both for occupational crime and for corporate crime at both the rotten apple level and the rotten barrel level.

Variety of White-Collar Crime

Miri-Lavassani et al. (2009) found that identity fraud is the fastest growing white-collar crime in many countries, especially in developed countries. In 2008, the number of identity fraud victims increased by 22% to 9.9 million victims.

Bank fraud is a criminal offence of knowingly executing a scheme to defraud a financial institution. For example in China, bank fraud is expected to increase both in complexity and in quantity as criminals keep upgrading their fraud methods and techniques. Owing to the strong penal emphasis of Chinese criminal law, harsh punishment including death penalty and life imprisonment has been used frequently for serious bank fraud and corruption. Cheng and Ma (2009) found, however, that the harshness of the law has not resulted in making the struggle against criminals more effective. The uncertain law and inconsistent enforcement practices have made offenders more fatalistic about the matter, simply hoping they will not be the unlucky ones to get caught.

Fraud is generally defined as the procurement of a private asset or means of advantage through deception or through the neglect of care for the interests of an asset required by duty. In particular, fraud includes heterogeneous forms such as misappropriation, balance manipulation, insolvency, and capital investment fraud (Füss and Hecker, 2008).

Corruption might be defined as the misuse of entrusted authority for personal benefit. Business corruption is defined by the involvement of private companies and is usually motivated by corporate profits. Søreide (2006) suggests that in contrast to the term "political corruption" or the term "petty corruption", where we focus on the interests of politicians or civil servants, we usually emphasize the perspectives and the interests of the bribers when applying the term "business corruption".

The problem of business corruption can be exemplified by a number of scandals. An example is Exxon Mobile in Kazakhstan, where payments were made to Kazakh officials to obtain a share in the Karachaganak oil and gas field. Another example is the Lesotho Dam project, in which eight international construction companies were charged with bribery after they allegedly paid bribes to win contracts for a large dam project. Yet another example is the Titan Corporation's unofficial payments to the President of Benin to get important business advantages (Søreide, 2006).

We are most accustomed to thinking about corrupt behavior in organizations primarily in micro level terms. Ashforth *et al.* (2008) argue that it is comforting to assume that one bad apple or renegade faction within an organization is somewhat responsible for the corruption we too often observe. However, organizations are important to our understanding of corruption, because they influence the actions of their members. Therefore, both micro and macro views are important to understand corruption.

Pinto *et al.* (2008) applied both views in their study of corruption. They focused on two fundamental dimensions of corruption in organizations: (i) whether the individual or the organization is the beneficiary of the corrupt activity and (ii) whether the corrupt behavior is undertaken by an individual actor or by two or more actors.

To enable a better understanding of the similarities, distinctions, frictions, and complementarities among corruption control types and to lay the groundwork for future study of their effectiveness in combination, Lange (2008) set forth a theoretical basis for considering a corruption control type in the context of other corruption control types.

Pfarrer *et al.* (2008) proposed a four-stage model of the organizational actions that potentially increase the speed and likelihood that an organization will restore its legitimacy with stakeholders following a transgression.

Misangyi *et al.* (2008) draw from theories of institutions and collective identities to present a threefold framework of institutional change — involving institutional logics, resources, and social actors — that furthers our understanding of the mitigation of corruption.

Corruption tends to have a deep impact on business corporations, business industries and society as a whole. Corruption has an important economic as well as social impact. Dion (2010) described corruption from three basic viewpoints: the structural perspective, the social-normative perspective, and the organizational-normative perspective. In the structural perspective, corruption is a local and domestic issue, so the best way to get rid of it is to have stronger laws and regulations. In the social-normative perspective, corruption is common wherever most of the people have dishonest practices and customs. Corruption is not perceived as an immoral behavior, since it has been socially institutionalized and tolerated by political authorities. In the organizational-normative perspective, corruption is dependent on organizational norms of behavior and may take on three different forms, i.e., procedural corruption, schematic corruption, and categorical corruption.

Collins *et al.* (2009) studied why firms engage in corruption in India. Building on a survey of 341 executives in India, they found that if executives have social ties with government officials, their firms are more likely to engage in corruption. Also, these executives are likely to reason that engaging in corruption is a necessity for being competitive.

White-collar crime is a broad concept that covers all illegal behavior that takes advantage of positions of professional authority and power as well as opportunity structures available within business for personal and corporate gain (Kempa, 2010: 252):

> Crimes such as embezzlement, fraud and insider trading, on one hand, and market manipulation, profit exaggeration, and product misrepresentation on the other, add up to a massive criminal domain.

White-collar crime contains several clear components (Pickett and Pickett, 2002):

➤ *It is deceitful.* People involved in white-collar crime tend to cheat, lie, conceal, and manipulate the truth.
➤ *It is intentional.* Fraud does not result from simple error or neglect but involves purposeful attempts to illegally gain an advantage. As such, it induces a course of action that is predetermined in advance by the perpetrator.

➤ *It breaches trust*. Business is based primarily on trust. Individual relationships and commitments are geared toward the respective responsibilities of all parties involved. Mutual trust is the glue that binds these relationships together, and it is this trust that is breached when someone tries to defraud another person or business.

➤ *It involves losses*. Financial crime is based on attempting to secure an illegal gain or advantage and for this to happen there must be a victim. There must also be a degree of loss or disadvantage. These losses may be written off or insured against or simply accepted. White-collar crime nonetheless constitutes a drain on national resources.

➤ *It may be concealed*. One feature of financial crime is that it may remain hidden indefinitely. Reality and appearance may not necessarily coincide. Therefore, every business transaction, contract, payment, or agreement may be altered or suppressed to give the appearance of regularity. Spreadsheets, statements, and sets of accounts cannot always be accepted at face value; this is how some frauds continue undetected for years.

➤ *There may be an appearance of outward respectability*. Fraud may be perpetrated by persons who appear to be respectable and professional members of society, who may even be employed by the victim.

PricewaterhouseCoopers (PwC) is a consulting firm conducting biennial global economic crime surveys. The 2007 economic crime study reveals that many things remain the same: globally, economic crime remains a persistent and intractable problem from which US companies are not immune as over 50% of US companies were affected by it in the past two years.

Percentage of companies reporting actual incidents of fraud according to PwC (2007) were:

➤ 75% suffered asset misappropriation
➤ 36% suffered accounting fraud

> ➤ 23% suffered intellectual property infringement
> ➤ 14% suffered corruption and bribery
> ➤ 12% suffered money laundering

Theories of White-Collar Crime

The *theory of embezzlement* suggests that a three-step process must be present for embezzlement to occur. First, the criminal perceives himself or herself as having a non-shareable financial problem. The person considers this financial problem to be one that cannot be shared with others, even if others could have helped. Next, the problem must be able to be secretly resolved by violation of the criminal's position of financial trust. There must be an opportunity for trust violation. Finally, the criminal is able to apply verbalizations to the conduct, which enable him or her to rationalize the conception of trusted person with the misuse of the entrusted funds or property. In this final phase, the trust violator defines the relationship between the non-shareable problem and the illegal solution in language that allows the criminal to look upon trust violation as essentially non-criminal, as justified, and as a part of a general irresponsibility for which he or she is not completely accountable (Ventura and Daniel, 2010).

Utility theory suggests that a criminal will attempt to maximize the utility from criminal behavior. An expected utility maximizing criminal commits an illegal act and, if he is not caught and punished, his total wealth thereby increases by an amount, x. His criminally enhanced total wealth, $w + x$, will be greater than his current wealth w. He is caught and punished with probability, p, and the punishment consists of a fine, z, which is less than or equal to his enhanced wealth, $w + x$. His personal assessment of any benefits to him of his criminal activity is described by a utility function linking p and z to w and x (Cain, 2009).

Fraud theory argues that three conditions of fraud are arising from fraudulent financial reporting (Ilter, 2009):

➢ Incentives/pressures: Management or other employees have incentives or pressures to commit fraud.
➢ Opportunities: Circumstances provide opportunities for management or employees to commit fraud.
➢ Attitudes/rationalization: An attitude, character, or set of ethical values exists that allows management or employees to intentionally commit a dishonest act, or an environment that imposes pressure sufficient to cause them to rationalize committing a dishonest act.

Thus, the risk of fraud is a combination of incentives/pressures, opportunities, and attitude/rationalization. The fraud examination process centers on the fraud hypothesis approach, which has four sequential steps (Ilter, 2009): analyzing the available data, developing a fraud hypothesis, revising it as necessary, and confirming it.

Detection of White-Collar Crime

White-collar crime can be difficult to detect, both by internal entities such as internal audit, and by external entities such as the stock exchange.

Kempa (2010) discussed reasons why white-collar crime is so difficult to detect and investigate by external entities. He identified the following four main reasons:

➢ *Obstacles to coordinated market enforcement and regulation.* Liberalism is the dominant political economic rationality for most Western governments. Liberalism holds the foundational value of private property as the space for individual liberty and desire not to interfere in market space beyond the bare minimum.
➢ *Structural issues.* Given the complexity of market processes, it is not surprising that the legal, regulatory and institutional systems that have grown up to regulate and police them are equally complicated. There are many authorities involved in securing markets and combating white-collar crime.

➢ *Legal issues*. Given the structural complexity of the networks for regulation, it follows that multiple nodes currently find themselves operating within multiple legal frameworks. This causes difficulties in sharing information, both for the reason that information sharing is sometimes expressly prohibited and for the reason that participants may be uncertain as to whether they may share information with a more powerful institutional player.

➢ *Cultural issues*. Given that the nodes in the contemporary regulatory and enforcement network represent the public, private, civil, and banking sectors, it is not surprising that they often hold different objectives, aligned with different worldviews, and have developed distinct skills and approaches that reflect those worldviews. For example, the emphasis by some corporations upon the need for quick recovery of the assets lost to white-collar crime can sometimes frustrate the broader preventive and rehabilitative objectives of justice, which can in turn work against ensuring the integrity of the enforcement system into the future.

A survey was conducted by the author of this book on white-collar crime issues in Norway. The five hundred and seventeen largest business companies in terms of annual turnover were identified in Norway for our empirical study of white-collar crime. A letter was mailed to the chief financial officer asking him or her to fill in the questionnaire to be found on a web site using a password found in the letter. The research was carried out via a web-based questionnaire combined with a letter to the largest business organizations in Norway.

65 respondents filled in the questionnaire after the first letter, 45 responses were received after a reminder, and another 31 responses were received after a second reminder. Thus, a total of 141 complete responses were received. 141 complete responses out of 517 potential responses represent a response rate of 27%. In addition, 36 incomplete responses were received, creating a gross

response rate of 34%. The survey web site was open to responses from January to April in 2010.

Separate analysis was conducted on the first set of responses, then the second set, and finally the third set was included. This analysis shows few changes in results when moving from 65 via 110 to 141 responses. Thus, the analysis suggests that non-respondents might have provided similar responses to actual respondents.

The average number of employees in the 141 business organizations with complete answers was 1,719 persons. The largest responding firm in terms of employees had 30,000 persons in its staff.

Respondents were asked to type in their current position, even though the letter was specifically mailed to the top executive in charge of finance, often called chief financial officer (CFO). Most of the respondents were indeed CFOs, but some were CEOs, corporate controllers, managers of finance, and chief group controllers.

The average age among respondents was 48 years among the first 65 responses, and they had 4.4 years of college and university education on average. The average age decreased to 46 years when the first reminder responses arrived, while the average education increased to 4.8 years. There were 91 men and 19 women responding after the first reminder letter. After two reminders, there were 116 male and 24 female chief financial officers in the sample.

The average age remained at 46 years after receipt of the final 31 responses, while average education continued to increase to 5.1 years. There were 117 men and 24 women among the total 141 respondents. The only change, therefore, seems to indicate that higher-educated persons tend to respond more frequently after reminders.

There was an open-ended question in the questionnaire concerned with challenges of white-collar crime detection. The question was formulated like this: *Why can it be difficult to detect, investigate and prosecute white-collar crime?*

Some respondents focused on the offender in their responses. Examples include:

> *"This kind of crime is committed by persons who have access to resources and who have rich knowledge of the business and know-how to hide tracks"*
> *"Executives are in charge of control mechanisms and management accounting. When they themselves commit financial crime, they manipulate internal control and management auditing"*
> *"Whistle-blowing to the top is risky, since the receiver of the message may be involved in the crime"*

Other respondents focused on the offense in their responses. Examples include:

> *"You need to get into the details, often single items in an invoice, to be able to detect misconduct. Very often it is difficult to find tracks in accounting systems"*
> *"It takes a long time to detect, so the offender has time to launder tracks"*
> *"Methods applied by criminal executives become more and more sophisticated"*

A third group of responses focused on shortcomings in control mechanisms. Examples include:

> *"International trade and transactions with a number of vendors and customers makes it extremely difficult for local auditors to follow paths from origin to destination"*
> *"We live in a society where we trust each other. We are not suspicious enough"*
> *"Internal control systems are often weak, and there is a lack of rules for top management"*

This classification of responses into three categories resulted from content analysis, where the three categories can be labeled as follows:

> ➢ *Criminal.* The white-collar criminal is in charge, has access to resources and has been trusted for too long.
> ➢ *Crime.* The white-collar crime is found in the details, and tracks have been laundered away before investigation starts.

➤ *Control*. Transactions across borders and accounting systems are difficult to detect by limited and deficient auditing procedures.

In addition, many respondents seem to indicate that there is an imbalance between control systems and trust, where control systems are deficient while trust is at an unreasonable high level. Top executives are trusted until there is concrete evidence internally or continued criticism externally.

As a consequence of criminal characteristics, crime characteristics, control characteristics and imbalance between control and trust, white-collar crime seems difficult to detect and investigate. A research model illustrating this causal relationship is shown in Figure 3.

Three hypotheses are implicit in the research model that might be explored in future research:

H1. *Higher competence by white-collar criminals causes increased complexity in crime investigation.*

H2. *More sophisticated white-collar crime causes increased complexity in crime investigation.*

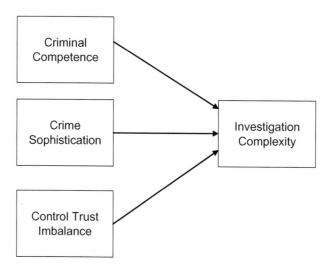

Figure 3.   Research Model Derived from Survey Responses.

H3. Greater imbalance between trust in white-collar employees and control of white-collar employees causes increased complexity in crime investigation.

Langfield-Smith and Smith (2003) introduced a framework for design of management control systems. This framework includes characteristics of the transaction, the actors, the environment, the control mechanisms, as well as trust. The framework seems to address many of the issues listed by respondents in our survey.

Hansen (2009) argues that prevention of corporate crime should not only be the concern of regulatory and law enforcement agencies. Corporations stand to lose more than reputation when financial scandals occur. Even when white-collar crime does not reach Royal Bank of Scotland, Enron or WorldCom proportions, corporations are damaged. It is estimated that white-collar crime can cost companies on average six percent of annual sales.

Three major reasons why white-collar crime is so hard to detect were identified in this research based on an opinion survey of chief financial officers. First, white-collar crime is often found in the details, making forensic evidence difficult to identify and present. While there is often a visible victim and offender in other types of crime, white-collar crime tends to cause damage to systems and organizations rather than individuals. Forensic evidence might be found in details such as invoices, bank accounts, and other transactions, but it is usually hard to detect (Chan *et al.*, 2008).

Next, white-collar criminals tend to be among the most knowledgeable and influential persons in the organization, thereby effectively preventing others from insights into the crime and actions against the criminal. White-collar criminals achieve obedience based on their authority in the workplace and the threat of losing one's job for failure to go along with the executive's scheme. Obedience theory posits that individuals may engage in behaviors that conflict with their personal values and beliefs if they are subjected to pressures to obey someone in authority (Baird and Zelin, 2009).

Finally, white-collar crime is so hard to detect because of control deficiencies in the company. Accounting and auditing, governance and compliance systems tend to be formal procedures rather than intelligence and investigation mechanisms. According to Hansen (2009), self-regulation in the form of corporate governance cannot alone prevent white-collar crime.

Chapter 2

Corporate Reputation

When a corporation is confronted by suspicions or allegations of business impropriety and white-collar crime, one of the most important intangible assets the company has to lose is its reputation in the marketplace and among other stakeholders (Hemphill, 2006). However, many organizations put the importance of a sound reputation to the back of their minds while they attend to operational tasks such as marketing and finance.

The importance of corporate reputation may vary with industry. In knowledge organizations where products are invisible, reputation can be more important than in manufacturing organizations, where products are visible. Knowledge-based organizations such as professional service firms in the consulting, legal, medical, educational and financial sectors seem extremely dependent on a good reputation to attract customers and clients.

A good reputation can lead to customer preference in doing business with the company when other companies' goods and services are available at a similar price and quality. A good reputation can enable the company to charge a premium for its products. A good reputation can enhance stakeholder support and loyalty.

Corporate Reputation Defined

Corporate reputation is an important asset or liability bestowed upon a corporation by its stakeholders (Love and Kraatz, 2009). Walker (2010) defined corporate reputation by making distinctions between organizational identity, organizational image and corporate reputation. Organizational identity is the most central, enduring, and distinctive basic character of an organization. Organizational image is outsider judgment based on perception of corporate communications. Corporate reputation represents what is actually known by both internal and external stakeholders. For example, stakeholders perceive a corporation to be corrupt or involved in other forms of white-collar crime.

Corporate reputation is a soft concept. It is the overall estimation and judgment of an organization that is held by its internal and external stakeholders based on the corporation's past actions and expected future actions and behavior. There may be differences in reputation among stakeholders according to their experiences and preferences in dealing with the organization as well as the information they have obtained from others.

Corporate reputation is the collective judgment of a corporation, it is a set of characteristics attributed to a firm by stakeholders, and it is visible in the particular type of feedback, received by the organization from its stakeholders, concerning the credibility of the organization's identity claims. However, reactions by stakeholders in relation to a firm are not part of the reputation (Einwiller *et al.*, 2010).

Corporate reputation is a perceptual representation of a company's past actions and future prospects that describe the firm's overall appeal to all its key constituents when compared to other leading rivals. Reputation is a combination of reality such as economic and social performance and perception such as performance perceived by key stakeholders (Hemphill, 2006).

Corporate reputation is a global and general, temporally stable, evaluative judgment about a corporation that is shared by multiple stakeholders. It is the net reaction of customers, investors, employees, and other stakeholders to the company. It is a collective of individual impressions (Highhouse *et al.*, 2009). Similarly, Friedman (2009) defines corporate reputation as a relatively stable, long-term intangible corporate asset that is important for organizational competitiveness. It is a perceptual representation of a company's past actions and future prospects that describe the company's overall appeal to all its key constituents when compared to its rivals.

Three key attributes are emphasized in the definition of reputation: (i) reputation is based on perceptions; (ii) it is the aggregate perception of all stakeholders; and (iii) it is comparative. Furthermore, (iv) reputation can be positive or negative; and (v) it is stable and enduring (Walker, 2010).

Awareness of the link between corporate reputation and white-collar crime has risen substantially in the business world after the joint collapse of Enron and Arthur Andersen. As a consequence, companies have become more sensitive to the value of their reputation. Corporate audiences, including institutional and individual investors, customers and suppliers, public authorities and competitors, evaluate the reputation of firms when making choices and other decisions (Linthicum *et al.*, 2010).

The two main sources of the corporate reputation are experience and information — a person's or group's past dealings with the company and the extent and nature of their direct and indirect communication with the company. It is argued that a favorable reputation requires not only an effective communications effort on the part of the corporation. More importantly, it requires an admirable identity that can be molded through consistent performance, usually over many years and even decades.

Resource-Based Theory

According to the resource-based view of the firm, corporate reputation can be considered to be a valuable strategic resource that contributes to or harms a corporation's sustainable position (Keh and Xie, 2009). The central tenet in resource-based theory is that unique organizational resources of both a tangible and intangible nature are the real source of competitive advantage. With resource-based theory, organizations are viewed as a collection of resources that are heterogeneously distributed within and across industries. Accordingly, what makes the performance of an organization distinctive is the unique blend of the resources it possesses.

Corporate reputation is an intangible resource that influences stakeholder behavior, including that of employees, management, customers and investors (Friedman, 2009). The resource-based view of the firm places specific emphasis on corporate intangibles that are difficult to imitate. Reputation is one corporate intangible that is thought to enhance customer satisfaction and loyalty, employee attraction and retention, firm equity, and investor awareness. It is also argued that reputation as a resource enhances bargaining power in trade channels, helps raise capital on the equity market, provides a second chance in the event of a crisis, provides access to the best professional service providers, facilitates new product introduction, and adds value such as trust to goods and services (Highhouse *et al.*, 2009).

Corporate reputation as an intangible resource is both influenced by the extent of white-collar crime as well as an influence on the extent of white-collar crime. Competitors that are involved in given value networks contribute to define how each enterprise in an industry can strive for profit. Dion (2009) argues that the capacity to convert corporate intangibles, such as corporate reputation, into a negotiable value could contribute to prevent corporate crime.

From a resource-based perspective, reputation is a valuable and rare resource that can lead to a sustained advantage or a temporary or permanent collapse. A good reputation is difficult to imitate and highly causally ambiguous. Walker (2010) argues that the greater the ambiguity experienced by constituents, the greater the importance of reputation as a resource as it reduces uncertainty by signaling, for example, service quality.

Although reputation is an intangible resource, it is argued that a good reputation consistently increases or sustains corporate worth and provides sustained competitive advantage. A business can achieve its objectives more easily if it has a good and consistent reputation among its stakeholders, especially key stakeholders such as its largest customers, opinion leaders in the business community, suppliers and current and potential employees.

Determinants of Corporate Reputation

In addition to white-collar crime, there are a number of other determinants of corporate reputation. For example, Highhouse *et al.* (2009: 1481) applied an organizational impression management perspective on the formation of corporate reputation by asking how reputation judgments are formed:

> What factors are considered? How can reputation judgments be influenced? These are questions that are appropriately addressed by behavioral science. Working from a view of reputation as a social construction — one that indicates the general, shared regard in which relevant constituents hold a company — we review literature that is relevant to the formation and foundation of corporate reputation.

Highhouse *et al.* (2009) applied a working definition of reputation as a collective of individual impressions that necessitated a micro view of impression formation as a foundation for understanding corporate reputation. In their search for determinants of corporate reputation, the researchers distinguished between internal and external factors, where internal factors were separated into substantive and symbolic attributes. Substantive attributes that may harm reputation in a similar way as white-collar crime are lack of social capital, lack of knowledge, lack of product development, and diversification with little substance. Symbolic attributes that may harm reputation in a similar way as white-collar crime are failed advertising, misleading public relations and negative corporate social responsibility policy. External factors that may harm reputation in a similar way as white-collar crime are negative word of mouth and negative media exposure.

In a different study, Friedman (2009) searched for determinants of corporate reputation within human resource management. He found that organizational value is lost when employee competencies and motivation deteriorate since this in turn negatively influences corporate reputation. He argues that effective implementation of the strategic partner, the change agent, the administrative expert and the employee champion human resources management roles can indirectly enhance corporate reputation.

Love and Kraatz (2009) focused only on downsizing as a determinant of corporate reputation. The aim of their study was to illuminate reputational change processes and identify the underlying theoretical mechanisms. They found that downsizing exerted a strong, negative effect on reputation, consistent with the character explanation.

Resource-based theory can be applied to understand the role of news media as an influence on corporate reputation. Corporate reputation is influenced by news media when stakeholders are dependent on news media to learn about reputation dimensions of the company. If stakeholders learn directly from experience and observation, then news media are less important. This is in line with media system dependency theory, which proposes an integral relationship among audiences, the news media and the larger social and economic system. Dependency is defined as a relationship in which the satisfaction of needs or the attainment of goals by one party is contingent upon the resources of another party (Einwiller *et al.*, 2010).

Effects of Corporate Reputation

According to Friedman (2009), corporate reputation is an intangible resource that influences stakeholder behavior, including that of employees, management, customers and investors. According to Highhouse *et al.* (2009), reputation is thought to enhance customer satisfaction and loyalty, employee attraction and retention, firm equity, and investor awareness. It is also argued that reputation as a resource enhances possibilities in a number of other aspects. According to Dion (2009), reputation can even prevent white-collar crime.

Keh and Xie (2009) studied how corporate reputation influences customer behavioral intentions. They proposed a model with customer trust, customer identification and customer commitment as the key intervening factors between corporate reputation and customer purchase intention and willingness to pay a price premium. They tested the model empirically and found that corporate reputation has positive influence on both customer trust and customer identification. Furthermore, customer commitment mediates the relationships between the two relational constructs (customer trust and customer identification) and behavioral intentions.

Theories of Corporate Reputation

In addition to resource-based theory, a number of other theories can be applied to examine corporate reputation. Examples include institutional theory, signaling theory, stakeholder theory, social identity theory, game theory, social cognition theory, economic theory, mass communication theory, impression management theory, and transaction cost theory (Walker, 2010).

To understand how the three most prominently used theoretical perspectives have been applied, Walker (2010) presented them as moving from pre-action, to action, and finally to post-action. With a focus on context and building reputation, institutional theory is often applied at the pre-action stage. The theory is used to examine how corporations gain legitimacy and cultural support within their institutional contexts to build their reputation.

At the action stage, signaling theory includes building images (signals), maintaining, and defending a reputation based on projected organizational images. The theory is applied to corporate reputation to explain how the strategic choices of firms represent signals, which are then used by stakeholders to form impressions of the firms. At the post-action stage, resource-based theory is applied to understand the outcome of a strong reputation. The theory examines how reputation is a valuable and rare resource that leads to a sustained competitive advantage (Walker, 2010).

The self-presentation theory suggests that corporations, like individuals, are concerned with the impression they create among stakeholders. According to Highhouse *et al.* (2009), there are two self-presentation motives of corporations: (i) desire for approval and (ii) desire for status. Like individuals, corporations develop reputations based on their success at getting along with others and getting ahead of others. This socio-analytical perspective of personality focuses on external perceptions where the structure of organizational personality is found in the structure of perceptions.

Measurement of Corporate Reputation

A construct such as corporate reputation must have an empirical operationalization closely tied to construct definition. Therefore, measurement of corporate reputation should examine perceived reputation in terms of stakeholders' perceptions, not factual representation. The perceptual nature of the construct reputation is important to measure correctly. There are three important considerations for measuring corporate reputation, i.e., reputation for-what, reputation for-whom, and reputation to-whom.

Reputation is a relative construct that can be relative to reputation in the past, relative to competitors at present, or relative to a desired or acceptable reputation level. Measurement of corporate reputation should therefore permit the construct to be both positive and negative.

A central theme in the reputation literature is the reasoning that stakeholders assign positive reputation to corporations that appear to possess desirable character traits. In this theme, stakeholders views organizations as coherent and purposive social entities rather than mere social aggregates or collectivities. Furthermore, constituencies are especially concerned with organizations' sustainability as partners. Therefore, stakeholders tend to admire corporations that appear to possess character traits such as trustworthiness and reliability (Love and Kraatz, 2009).

Rebuilding Corporate Reputation

Rebuilding corporate reputation involves both transparency and action. As argued by Bonini *et al.* (2009), reputation is built on a foundation not only of communications but also of deeds. Sharing information about critical business issues is important, and reputation-oriented actions such as willingness to tackle white-collar crime have to be convincing to stakeholders.

When a company responds to serious reputation threats from white-collar crime, the company must use many other means in addition to formal marketing and public relations. Such means of spreading positive messages about its activities quickly include the asking of people with high standing to reinforce key strategic messages, interactive web sites, and credible third parties speaking for the company (Bonini *et al.*, 2009).

Dowling (2006: 98) argues that corporate reputation is best communicated through stories, where good corporate stories and reputation are built on a solid platform of valued mission and good morality and behavior:

> This information should be crafted into a corporate reputation story sustainable for both internal and external stakeholders. Corporate reputation storytelling in its long forms (such as books, shareholder briefings, advertorials, web sites, and annual reports) and short forms (in corporate advertising) is art underpinned by science. The art of storytelling involves creating enough mystery

and intimacy to result in a more favorable evaluation of the company.

Brønn and Vidaver-Cohen (2009) studied corporate motives for social initiative. They studied motives such as legitimacy, sustainability and bottom line for engaging in social initiatives. Of the four motives in the legitimacy factor applied, they found that the motives to improve image and to be recognized for moral leadership dominated the list. Furthermore, sustainability motives for social initiative were driven by personal managerial values, while profitability motives were driven by the belief that engaging in social initiatives can yield direct financial benefits for the firm, either by generating new revenues or by protecting existing profit levels.

Social Responsibility and Corporate Reputation

In the three stage model of corporate social responsibility developed by Castello and Lozano (2009), corporate reputation is important as a fundamental requirement at the first stage. Stage 1, labeled risk management, is a base stage where corporate social responsibility is seen as a tool to protect reputation value. Within the risk management stage, firms start to develop systems to measure and control environmental and social issues and threats. These control systems involve planning and social forecasting, preparation for social response and development of the first set of corporate social policies.

Corporate social responsibility is tightly linked to acceptable ethical behavior, since it represents the continuing commitment by businesses to behave ethically and contribute to economic development while improving the quality of life of the workforce as well as the community at large (Linthicum *et al.*, 2010).

Linthicum *et al.* (2010) examined the influence of social responsibility on firm reputation during a period of crises. Specifically, they studied the influence of social responsibility ratings on market returns to Arthur Andersen clients following the Enron audit failure. Proponents of social responsibility argue that social responsibility can improve the reputation of the firm, while detractors argue that social responsibility expenditures are a poor use of shareholder money. Results from the study were inconsistent with claims that social responsibility can burnish a firm's reputation in a time of crises and with prior research indicating a positive relationship between social responsibility and market value. This is because the researchers found no evidence that social responsibility mitigated the negative returns to Arthur Andersen clients following the Enron audit failure. The researchers used a matched sample of Arthur Andersen and non-Arthur Andersen firms.

Corporate Governance Ratings

An influential factor on corporate reputation from a white-collar perspective is corporate governance rating. Corporate governance ratings can be based on categories such as board, audit, charter, executive compensation, and director education. Governance ratings can be generated from reviews of public and private corporate information, as well as from interviews with top executives and independent trustees. Such ratings can be influential, for example, with investors on matters related to election of directors and executive compensation. Corporate governance scores can also influence credit rating services, thereby directly impacting cost of capital (Abdolmohammadi and Read, 2010).

Abdolmohammadi and Read (2010) studied the relationship between corporate governance ratings and the incidence of financial restatement. They selected a sample of 150 US firms that restated their financial statements for 2003 to bring them into conformity with general accounting principles. The researchers found that the sample of restatements had significantly lower governance ratings than the control sample during the restated year of 2003. They also found that the sample of restatement firms improved their governance ratings in the year following the restated year, suggesting that financial restatement leads to improvements in governance mechanisms.

Chapter 3

Reputation Damage and Repair

It seems to be a common view that white-collar crime scandals can cause serious damage to company reputation. Even when white-collar crime does not reach Royal Bank of Scotland, Enron, Siemens or WorldCom proportions, research literature suggests that corporate reputation is damaged (Carnegie and Napier, 2010; Einwiller *et al.*, 2010; Hansen, 2009; James and Seipel, 2010; Keh and Xie, 2009; Linthicum *et al.*, 2010; Love and Kraatz, 2009; Pearson, 2010; Walker, 2010; Weissmann, 2009).

Based on a survey of opinions among chief financial officers presented in this chapter, there seems to be a consensus indeed that corporate reputation is hurt when white-collar crime in the organization has been revealed. However, the damage in terms of both extent and duration might vary depending on several contingency factors. One contingency factor is whether the company is perceived as an offender or a victim.

Reputation Survey Design

The five hundred and seventeen largest business companies in terms of annual turnover were identified in Norway for our empirical study of white-collar crime. A letter was mailed to the chief financial officer asking him or her to fill in the questionnaire to be found on a web site using a password found in the letter. The research was carried out via a web-based questionnaire combined with a letter to the largest business organizations in Norway.

65 respondents filled in the questionnaire after the first letter, 45 responses were received after a reminder, and another 31 responses were received after a second reminder. Thus, a total of 141 complete responses were received. 141 complete responses out of 517 potential responses represent a response rate of 27%. In addition, 36 incomplete responses were received, creating a gross response rate of 34%. The survey web site was open to responses from January to April in 2010.

Separate analysis was conducted on the first set of responses, then the second set, and finally the third set was included. This analysis shows few changes in results when moving from 65 via 110 to 141 responses. Thus, the analysis suggests that non-respondents might have provided similar responses to actual respondents.

The average number of employees in the 141 business organizations with complete answers was 1719 persons. The largest responding firm in terms of employees had 30000 persons in its staff.

Respondents were asked to type in their current position, even though the letter was specifically mailed to the top executive in charge of finance, often called the chief financial officer (CFO). Most of the respondents were indeed CFOs, but some were CEOs, corporate controllers, managers of finance, and chief group controllers.

The average age among respondents was 48 years among the first 65 responses, and they had 4.4 years of college and university education on average. The average age decreased to 46 years when the first reminder responses arrived, while the average education increased to 4.8 years. There were 91 men and 19 women responding after the first reminder letter. After two reminders, there were 116 male and 24 female chief financial officers in the sample.

The average age remained at 46 years after receipt of the final 31 responses, while average education continued to increase to 5.1 years. There were 117 men and 24 women among the total 141 respondents. The only change, therefore, seems to indicate that higher-educated persons tend to respond more frequently after reminders.

Reputation Survey Results

The open-ended question in the questionnaire to the CFO about potential effect of white-collar crime on company reputation was formulated as: *How might the reputation of a company be affected in your opinion if it becomes evident that the company is involved in white-collar crime?* A total of 113 chief financial officers responded to this question. Responses were classified by applying content analysis (Riffe and Freitag, 1997).

Since there was an open-ended question in the questionnaire about how the company might be affected, each respondent provided an answer consisting of few words or complete sentences. Here are some examples:

> *"It depends on the type of business. For some organizations it can be completely devastating. Example: Arthur Andersen & Co that was terminated worldwide because of links to the Enron scandal. For other companies it hurts, but not so bad, especially if it turns out than individual employees in isolation were abusing their positions. It is much worse if the crime reflects the organizational culture"*
>
> *"Reputation is harmed if there is a common culture for these types of actions. If it is a single isolated incident, then it will probably not have any significant effect on company reputation"*
>
> *"Depending on what kind of company, it can certainly harm reputation. Statoil survives some misconduct linked to corruption and exploitation rights because it does not influence the real value of the company that is found in oil and gas reserves. For an auditing firm, however, it may be the certain death since the firm is completely dependent on its trustworthiness"*
>
> *"Not really. We work in the building and construction industry where expectations are lower than in other industries. In our company we do probably have an ethical standard that is far above the normal in our industry"*

Most respondents seemed to agree that company reputation would have to suffer damage from white-collar crime. However, as the last quote illustrates, not all respondents agree. While some respondents suggest that white-collar crime can kill the business, others suggest that there is minor effect that is forgotten after a short while.

Some respondents mentioned organizational culture. Organizational culture refers to shared assumptions, values, and norms. It is beliefs, values, and expectations held by organizational members. (Zheng *et al.*, 2010).

Contingent Perspectives

Many respondents present a contingent view, where the effect on reputation from white-collar crime is dependent on the situation. Some mention US examples of Andersen and Enron and local Norwegian examples such as Finance Credit and Sponsor Service, where the firms went out of business after the scandal. Others argue that reputation damage is both limited and short lived.

The contingent approach suggested by many respondents indicate that white-collar crime is more serious for company reputation if the crime reflects company culture, if the company is an offender rather than a victim, if it has happened in the company before, if the crime is considered very serious, if the company rather than an individual is considered to be the criminal, if the company is in service rather than goods production, and if local and national media find it interesting and relevant to report the case for a long time.

The contingent approach also implies that the damage to reputation can be reduced depending on how well the crisis is handled. If the company is open about it, shows willingness to sort things out and demonstrate results in terms of ethical standards and performance, then the damage may be temporary in nature. Most respondents seem to agree that damage in reputation will have a direct effect on the financial performance of the company, for example, in terms of lost sales and shareholder value.

When reading responses, it is interesting to interpret whether the company perceives itself as an offender or as a victim. Most of the responses indicating offender tend to suggest more serious consequence for reputation, while those indicating victim tend to suggest less serious consequence for the reputation. Overall, most of

Figure 1.   Causal Relationships between Determinants, Reputation and Effects.

the respondents assumed an offender situation rather than a victim situation. This is very different from earlier questions presented in this book that were related to prevention and detection, where most respondents assumed a victim situation for the company.

Contingent factors influence both determinants of corporate reputation as well as reputation effects from crime, as illustrated in Figure 1, and discussed in the following.

Crime Determinants of Reputation

As defined by Highhouse *et al.* (2009), reputation is a collective of individual impressions that necessitates a micro view of impression formation as a foundation for understanding corporate reputation. From the CFO responses, we see that the individual's assessment of crime reputation damage varies to a large extent. Based on this variation, we can also assume that individual impressions will vary significantly. The collective of CFO responses therefore reflects the collective of individual impressions.

Friedman (2009) searched for determinants of corporate reputation within human resource management. He found that organizational value is lost when employee competencies and motivation deteriorate since this in turn negatively influences corporate reputation. In this line of thinking, CFO responses suggest that employee motivation in particular deteriorate in periods of white-collar crime detection and attention. When employee motivation deteriorates, then human resources deteriorate, and so does corporate reputation.

Love and Kraatz (2009) focused only on downsizing as a determinant of corporate reputation. The aim of their study was to illuminate reputational change processes and identify the underlying theoretical mechanisms. In this line of thinking, CFO responses indicate that a business organization can be seriously hurt from white-collar crime and thus have to downsize. Such downsizing can exert a strong, negative effect on reputation, consistently with the character explanation.

Resource-based theory can be applied to understand the role of news media as an influence on corporate reputation. Corporate reputation is influenced by news media when stakeholders are dependent on news media to learn about reputation dimensions of the company. In this line of thinking, CFO responses indicate that media attention to white-collar crime has an important effect on corporate reputation. However, if stakeholders learn directly from experience and observation, then news media are less important. This is in line with media system dependency theory, which proposes an integral relationship among audiences, the news media and the larger social and economic system. Dependency is defined as a relationship in which the satisfaction of needs or the attainment of goals by one party is contingent upon the resources of another party (Einwiller *et al.*, 2010).

One of the CFO quotes above suggests that reputation is harmed if there is a common culture for these types of actions. If it is a single isolated incident then the respondent argues that it will probably not have any significant effect on company reputation.

Bucy *et al.* (2008) studied how to keep corporations from being indicted in terms of strategies a corporation facing potential prosecution should adopt to minimize exposure. Study participants' advice fell into three categories: (1) the importance of cooperating with the government, (2) distinguishing individuals from the corporate entity; and (3) pursuing and demonstrating internal efforts to address the wrongdoings. Full cooperation by the corporation with police and prosecuting authority might be necessary to avoid prosecution or reduce its impact. By separating the corporation from potentially culpable employees, the company is able to isolate incidents and potentially demonstrate that there was no knowledge or approval from upper management.

The extent of company reputation damage by white-collar crime is dependent on how the company responds. If the white-collar crime can be classified as a disaster, social research has focused on six different behavioral aspects of disasters. Perhaps the most frequently used term in connection with disasters is the word "panic". Collective panic might occur in disaster situations, especially when there is a perception of an immediate great threat to self and/or significant others. The second aspect is antisocial behavior, especially looting, that may occur in a disaster. The third aspect is passivity in emergencies, and remaining aspects in the work by Quarantelli (2008) are role conflict and role abandonment, sudden and widespread mental health breakdowns, and the locus of problems where the general belief is that the major source of problems and difficulties are the individuals involved.

The chief characteristic of corporations that encourage or discourage white-collar crime identified by Bucy *et al.* (2008) is leadership from the top that sets the tone for corporate behavior. An independent and active board of directors is the key component to healthy corporate governance. To help ensure the independence of directors, some companies require the election of at least one new director every year. Boards have to appoint more robust committees that are actively involved in oversight of all aspects of a corporation. For a board to truly monitor a corporation's financial status and eliminate incentives, an internal audit committee should regularly review both the company's financial statements and reports from its independent auditors.

Reputation Effects from Crime

According to Friedman (2009), corporate reputation is an intangible resource that influences stakeholder behavior, including that of employees, management, customers and investors. In the survey,

6 out of 113 CFOs mentioned explicitly customers, where relationship to customers can be damaged as well as customers lost. The same number of CFOs mentioned employees, where employee proudness of the company and motivation for the company deteriorates.

According to Highhouse *et al.* (2009), reputation is thought to enhance customer satisfaction and loyalty, employee attraction and retention, firm equity, and investor awareness. The opposite effect is expected when white-collar crime causes reputation decline. In the survey, firm equity and investor awareness are mentioned in one of the CFO responses that the effect from white-collar crime would be "lower market value on the stock exchange because of breach of trust".

It is also argued that reputation as a resource enhances possibilities in a number of other aspects (Dion, 2009). The opposite, of course, is a reduction in possibilities when reputation declines from white-collar crime. One CFO mentioned negative consequences for relationships to banks and credit insurance firms. Another CFO mentioned the ability to be a trustworthy partner in business ventures.

Keh and Xie (2009) studied how corporate reputation influences customer behavioral intentions. They proposed a model with customer trust, customer identification and customer commitment as the key intervening factors between corporate reputation and customer purchase intention and willingness to pay a price premium. 8 out of 113 CFOs mentioned the term "customer trust" explicitly in their responses. They said that "trust is alpha and omega" and that "trust is extremely important".

Keh and Xie (2009) tested their model empirically and found that corporate reputation has positive influence on both customer trust and customer identification. Furthermore, customer commitment mediates the relationships between the two relational constructs (customer trust and customer identification) and behavioral intentions.

While almost all responding chief financial officers suggest a negative effect from white-collar scandal on company reputation, the magnitude and duration of such an effect varies depending on the situation.

Rebuilding corporate reputation involves both transparency and action. As argued by Bonini *et al.* (2009), reputation is built on a foundation not only of communications but also of deeds. Sharing information about critical business issues is important, and reputation-oriented actions such as willingness to tackle white-collar crime have to be convincing to stakeholders.

Organizational culture can be both a barrier to and an enabler of reputation repair. Organizational culture refers to shared assumptions, values, beliefs, and expectations in an organization. If these values are positive and consistently held by organizational members, then the likelihood of reputation repair is fair. Furthermore, involvement is needed, where involvement is defined as the participation by an organization's members in decision making (Zheng *et al.*, 2010).

Ethics in Repair and Prevention

The importance of ethics is often stressed when it comes to preventing white-collar crime. Ethics has to do with examining and judging attitudes, behaviors and practices, as well as moral judgments, critically and often academically. Ethics also has to do with suggesting justified solutions to moral conflicts. Applied ethics means focusing on a more limited area — such as leadership in an occupation. Occupational ethics is about moral conflict management and moral criticism, as well as self-criticism related to work roles (Brinkmann and Henriksen, 2008).

Whilst ethics encompasses the system of beliefs that supports a particular view of morality, moralities are systems of rules of conduct that are developed to provide guidance in social and interpersonal behavior. These systems are used to regulate and moderate human affairs. Ethics involves the study of the tendency to do right or wrong, while morality refers to the standards of behavior by which people are judged in their relationships with others (Ho and Wong, 2008).

Corporate crime can reflect the normative structure of a given industry, that is, the normative commonly ethical norms. This is because enterprises within a specific industry often face common constraints and sources of uncertainty. Corporate executives tend to develop common attitudes toward and mutual concern with the constraints of their industry. Therefore, improving the contents of the ethical climate in an industry could reduce the occurrence of corporate crime (Dion, 2008).

Business organizations are developing codes of ethics, monitoring the ethical judgment of their managers, and training them in ethical decision making. But Dion (2008) argues that the real effectiveness of such ethical management strategies should be assessed within the context of the ethical climate that characterizes the organization itself. Crime prevention depends on the fact that the type of ethical climate will actually match with the ethical management strategies that are used. There is also a need for ethical fit between an organization's ethical strategy and its existing systems, structures, policies, procedures, and culture.

Rok (2009) studied ethical values in leading responsible organizations. He analyzed the effective and ethical leadership and the critical role of employees' participation in implementing corporate responsibility agenda. He found both to be of crucial importance for organizational change. Effective leadership can be the product of a group of people working together, to provide direction for the organization. People are responsible for the free choices they make. The attraction to the participative practices can nourish tendencies toward citizen involvement in other arenas as well. Like citizen participation is the basis of a working democracy, employee participation is the basis of a socially responsible company. Ethical values have to work in harmony and not contradict corporate culture values (Bucy *et al.*, 2008).

Bucy *et al.* (2008) found that inside and outside corporate counsel and independent auditors play increasingly important roles in verifying ethical and legal compliance. The key to deterring and detecting white-collar crime is effective corporate governance.

Brønn and Vidaver-Cohen (2009) studied corporate motives for social initiative. They studied motives such as legitimacy, sustainability and bottom line for engaging in social initiatives. Of the four motives in the legitimacy factor applied, they found that the motives to improve image and to be recognized for moral leadership dominated the list. Furthermore, sustainability motives for social initiative were driven by personal managerial values, while profitability motives were driven by the belief that engaging in social initiatives can yield direct financial benefits for the firm, either by generating new revenues or by protecting existing profit levels.

Investigating or Reporting

The extent of reputational damage is influenced by the way the organization reacts to suspicion and detection of white-collar crime. It can be smart to initiate corporate internal investigation to demonstrate willingness and interest in detecting and providing evidence that can later be valuable in internal sanctions as well as for external sanctions and possible court proceedings. Such willingness, interest and initiative might prove valuable in preventing reputation collapse and stimulate reputation recovery.

In the survey research, an open-ended question in the questionnaire to the CFO was concerned with actions on suspicion of white-collar crime and was formulated as follows: *How will you proceed upon suspicion of white-collar crime in your company?*

A total 109 respondents (out of 141) filled in their replies to this question. After applying content analysis to the responses (Riffe and Freitag, 1997), responses could be classified into three main categories:

1. *Reporting.* 64 out of 109 respondents will inform internally and/or externally, thus 59% for communication. The CFO might report to management above and/or the board, involve external auditors and investigators, involve the police in serious cases, report to internal audit team in the corporation, notify corporate compliance unit, inform control committee, follow whistle-blowing routines, inform executive in charge of ethics, use crime hotline if available, inform chief of security, work to provide forensic evidence, and involve internal control unit.
2. *Investigating.* 43 out of 109 respondents will investigate the case, thus 38% for investigation. The CFO might investigate and check facts, discuss with trusted colleagues and outside consultants, observe behavior, check documents, create a potential situation for the suspect, work with close subordinates on the case, and check accounting and invoicing for suspicious transactions or manipulated transactions.
3. *Confronting.* 3 out of 109 respondents will confront the suspect, thus 3% for confrontation. The CFO might dismiss the suspect from the company and report the case to police.

It may seem surprising that so many, 59%, choose reporting and informing others as their initial response to suspicion of white-collar crime in the company. This seems like a passive response, where the problem is moved to someone else. At the same time, it is a sign of caution. The fact that very few initially choose confronting the suspect is yet another sign of caution. However, we do think that an initial investigation might be the most appropriate response in many situations. It does not help to spread unsubstantiated rumors. Rather, rumors can be checked before they are passed on to others as more than rumors.

As argued by Hemphill (2006), corporate internal investigation as a reaction to white-collar crime allegations is an important move in protecting corporate reputation. He found that an interactive and reactive engagement approach requires explicit managerial recognition of the benefits.

Sequence of Actions

While our survey findings represent the distribution of initial response to suspicion of white-collar crime in business organizations, it might also be interesting to think about the sequence of responses. If there is a sequence, a choice can be made by the CFO between 1-2-3 and 1-3-2 if informing is first. After informing others (1), the CFO may collaborate with those others to investigate the case (2) and eventually confront the suspect (3). Or, after informing (1) and confronting (3) without success, further investigations may take place (2).

If investigating (2) is first, we may find sequences like 2-1-3 and 2-3-1, where informing or confronting occur as a second or third step. Finally, we may have confronting (3) first, where the suspect denies all allegations in an untrustworthy way, leading to communication and investigation, either as 3-2-1 or 3-1-2.

In fact, there may be a cyclical rather than a sequential procedure over time, where one activity is followed by another activity, and where the first activity returns again, as illustrated in Figure 2. For example, after initial investigations, preliminary information is communicated to the board, followed by further investigations by the CFO.

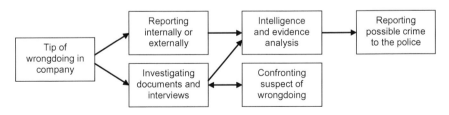

Figure 2.   Possible Sequence of Actions on Suspicion of White-Collar Crime.

In investigations, it is important to separate the path to find out the facts and the path to find the offender(s). It can be wise to start by searching the facts. Then, after the facts and evidence is ready, suspects can be made accountable for the crime. People tend to talk if it is about the case, and they become reluctant to talk if it is about guilt.

Chapter 4

Internal Investigations

An internal investigation has to be conducted properly and requires that the investigator acts thoughtfully and deliberately. An investigator that is not rash and arbitrary, but thorough and careful, is more likely to be considered fair. Internal investigations are helpful in uncovering critical information about misconduct and crime as well as accusations not rooted in reality. Neuser (2005) argues that internal investigations create an employee perception of professional employee relations. Employees understand that the organization has in-house competency in investigating and addressing incidents of unacceptable workplace conduct.

Corporate Investigation

Neuser (2005) makes suggestions for how to conduct the internal investigation. First, the investigator is responsible for gathering all facts relevant to the complaint in terms of tangible evidence and thoroughly questioning the complainant, the accused, and all relevant witnesses. This investigator also documents the investigation by preparing necessary investigative reports. Next, the art of asking the right questions includes knowing what questions to ask and knowing how to ask questions. The investigator needs to adopt an appropriate investigative style, be prepared to ask all the right questions, use the process of goal-orientation in investigative interviewing, and avoid the danger of compound questions. Finally, the investigator needs to be familiar with practical tools to help measure witness credibility and get close to the truth. Practical tools include asking the same question in various and different forms, asking for reasons (causality), and interpretation of silence.

Investigation Approaches

Neuser (2005) suggests 12 steps of an effective internal investigation:

Step 1: Interview the complainant

Step 2: Carefully document the complaint and plan the investigation

Step 3: Determine whether the complainant allegations require immediate intervention

Step 4: Inform the accused's supervisor about the complaint

Step 5: Determine whether the complaint allegations, if true, violate a company work rule, policy, or procedure

Step 6: Interview all potential witnesses

Step 7: Interview the accused

Step 8: Review the accused's personnel file

Step 9: Document the totality of the internal investigation

Step 10: Decide whether the objectionable conduct did occur and determine appropriate corrective action

Step 11: Inform all interested parties of the investigation's conclusions

Step 12: Create a final investigative file.

Hemphill and Cullari (2009) argue that when warranted by the gravity of allegations, the use of corporate internal investigations is a required activity. It should be an integral part of an organizational compliance and ethics program, rather than an optional initiative, by executives who are not the subject of suspicion. Having a formal corporate internal investigation mechanism in place will provide further evidence that a company is paying attention to compliance and ethics in terms of uncovering potential criminal malfeasance, can halt such alleged activity, and self-report this internal investigation.

An investigative approach available to CFOs is forensic accounting. Forensic accounting is concerned with identifying, recording, settling, extracting, sorting, reporting, and verifying past financial data. The focus of forensic accounting is on evidence revealed by the examination of financial documents. The evidence collected or prepared by a forensic accountant may be applied in different contexts. For example, forensic accounting results can serve as evidence in an internal corporate investigation that leads only to internal discipline, or no action whatever. Forensic results can also serve as evidence in a professional disciplinary hearing or other administrative proceedings, such as an administrative enforcement procedure by financial authorities. As evidence in some phase of a criminal action, the weight of that testimony will depend on a number of factors, the most important of which according to Curtis (2008) is whether the forensic accountant can be qualified as an expert and whether the opinion the accountant seeks to proffer actually qualifies as an expert opinion. When forensic accounting is applied as document study, it is typically combined with interviews and observations, thereby integrating behavioral aspects into forensic accounting (Ramamoorti, 2008). Forensic accounting is emerging as a specialist discipline (Kranacher *et al.*, 2008).

The majority of respondents in our survey suggest informing internally and/or externally. When informing externally, typical examples are external auditing, law firm or accounting firm. Very few mention the police, and it creates the impression that many respondents would like to avoid the police in situations of white-collar crime suspicion. This impression is in line with a research finding in Canada, where there are very strong incentives not to cooperate with the police. According to Williams (2008), cooperating with the police may subject both individuals and the company to the added jeopardy of regulatory scrutiny and class action lawsuits, as information revealed to the police may be used to support actions in other juridical settings. Individuals can be more worried about civil litigation than the criminal investigation because the civil litigation can cost them so much. They may, for example, be fearful of losing their jobs.

Why so few mention the police, might also be explained by how criminal investigations are sometimes implemented by police detectives. Attanasio (2008: 56) argues that bringing in the police will drive the corporation on the defense:

> The nightmare can begin in several ways. It could be a federal grand jury subpoena directed at the company's accounting or con-tracting practices. It could be the execution of a search warrant at the corporate headquarters or at an executive's home. It could be a phone call from a panicked employee who was just visited by Federal Bureau of Investigation agents. It could even begin as a news report confirmed by "unnamed sources" describing an investigation of a firm.

No matter how criminal investigations starts, Attanasio (2008) argues that the days, months and even years that follow can resem-ble a Kafkaesque drama of unprecedented stress, expense and public humiliation. It can end in lengthy jail sentences on fallen executives who become virtual household names for core criminals.

Based on this perspective, Attanasio (2008) indicates a very different answer to our research question: *How will you proceed on sus-picion of white-collar crime in your company?* His answer to the question of how a financial executive such as the CFO should handle criminal investigations by the police is very much characterized by the police being an enemy rather than an ally. The recommendation to the CFO is: (i) stop talking, (ii) don't touch evidence, and (iii) prepare for the worst.

Who to inform will depend on who is in the suspicion picture. Individuals or groups in the suspicion picture will not be informed, because they will have a subjective rather than objective opinion, and they will tend to manipulate and change facts. If the chief executive officer (CEO) is in the suspicion picture, all people who are close to the CEO might be avoided. People close to the CEO may be top management as well as the board, especially if the CEO is also a member of the board.

Often it will be difficult to find an independent person or body internally when the CEO is the potential criminal. Therefore, external communication can be more appropriate. The external auditor in an auditing firm can be contacted, so can an external law firm. However, if the CEO has strong links to these firms as well, the only feasible solution would be to contact the police. An advantage of informing the police is that information is passed on and stored in a law enforcement agency that cannot be manipulated by the CEO or any other company representative. A disadvantage of contacting the police, is that as mentioned above, Williams (2008) argues that cooperating with the police may subject both individuals and the company to the added jeopardy of regulatory scrutiny and class action lawsuits, as information revealed to the police may be used to support actions in other juridical settings.

Nevertheless, contacting the police in countries where the police is characterized by integrity and accountability is a safe procedure. Integrity is defined as the quality of being honest and morally upright, while accountability refers to situations in which someone is required or expected to justify actions or decisions (UNODC, 2006). Integrity in public office demands open and transparent decision making and clarity about the primacy of a public official's duty to serve the public interest above all else. Conflict between this duty and a person's individual interests cannot always be avoided but must always be identified, declared and managed in a way that stands up to scrutiny. This particularly applies to police officers who are sworn to uphold the law (OPI, 2007). Police integrity is an important element of what is called public integrity. According to Fijnaut and Huberts (2002), public integrity denotes the quality of acting in accordance with the moral values, norms and rules accepted by the body politic and the public. A number of integrity violations or forms of public misconduct can be distinguished: corruption including bribery, nepotism, cronyism, patronage; fraud and theft;

conflict of interest through assets, jobs and gifts; manipulation of information; discrimination and sexual harassment; improper methods for noble causes; the waste and abuse of resources; and private time misconduct.

Investigator Performance

An investigator who is searching for evidence examines records, develops chains of evidence, searches alternative explanations, makes judgments and prepares notes and reports. An investigator also interviews witnesses, victims, and suspects. In addition, an investigator collaborates with trusted colleagues and expertise to exchange information and coordinate activities.

To be a good investigator requires detective skills. According to Tong (2007), the secretive nature of the detective world has attracted little attention from researchers. However, competing perspectives about detective work can be discerned from available literature. Detective work has been characterized as an art, a craft, a science, and a combination of all three. The old regime of the seasoned detective highlighted the notion of detective work as a craft. An alternative perspective highlights the scientific nature of detective work, which focuses on the skills needed for crime scene management, the use of physical evidence, investigative interviewing, informant handling, offender profiling, management of the investigative process, and knowledge management.

It is important for detectives to be effective in their work, as new public management is focusing closely on the effective use of resources. However, measuring effectiveness is no easy task. Measurement, in an investigative context, has focused upon the outcome of cases, often at the expense of evaluating the process of the investigation and quality of its outputs. Tong (2007) argues that not only have the police been subject to inadequate measurement criteria such as clear-up rates, there has also been a lack of recognition of good quality police work. The task of recognizing good detective work involves more than providing an appropriate method of measurement; it also implies an awareness of the impact of practice as well as an awareness of the knowledge accumulation, sharing and reuse.

It follows that the most useful approach to measuring detective effectiveness will not necessarily be the measurement of specific outcomes, although such measures will be useful for resource management. Tong (2007) argues that effectiveness in the context of detective work is best measured by focusing on the key processes and decisions in which detectives engage to encourage a professional working culture based on how detectives come to decisions. In the context of the value shop for knowledge work, decisions are made in all five primary activities: understanding the problem, identifying problem solutions, prioritizing actions, implementing investigation, and evaluating and controlling detective work.

There are a number of factors that influence the effectiveness, performance and success of an investigator. First, the investigator should be curious. He or she should wonder what, how and why something has happened. To find out, the investigator needs a cognitive ability to learn through acquisition of facts, procedures and rules specific to the job. Furthermore, the investigator needs conscientiousness, neuroticism (emotional stability), extraversion, agreeableness, and openness to experience. Furthermore, there is a need for emotional intelligence, which is the ability to perceive accurately, appraise, and express emotions, as well as the ability to access and generate feelings when they facilitate thought.

Performance of an investigator can be measured in the steps suggested by Neuser (2005). Already in the first step of interviewing the complainant, personal qualifications of the investigator are exposed. The internal complaint determines the resulting investigation. Only by means of a conscious communication style will a complainant be willing and able to present the case in an optimal way. The investigator's style should facilitate the free flow of information. It is the investigator's job to guide the complainant carefully to disclose all of the complaint facts.

Investigator as Detective

Tong (2007) constructed the following profile of an effective detective after analyzing the academic literature relating to detective skills and abilities:

1. *Personal Qualities.* Intelligence, common sense, initiative, inquisitiveness, independence of thought, commitment, persistence, ability to talk to people, flexibility, ability to learn, reflexivity, lateral thinking, creative thinking, patience, empathy, tolerance and ability to interpret uncertain and conflicting information, ability to work away from family and home, interpret feelings, ideas and facts, honesty and integrity.
2. *Legal knowledge.* Knowledge of the law referring to police powers, procedure, criminal justice process, a good grounding in criminal law, awareness of changes to legislation, courtroom protocol, rules of disclosure, use of evidence, format of case file and awareness of defense arguments.
3. *Practical knowledge.* Technology available to detectives and used by criminals, understanding the context in which crime is committed and awareness of investigative roles of different functions of the police organization and specialist advisors. Recognition that crime changes with time and place and may require police responses that are tailored to specific contexts. Forensic awareness and practical expertise (e.g., crime scene preservation and packaging of evidence).
4. *Generic knowledge.* Recognition that knowledge changes, awareness of developments in practice will allow the detective to remain up to date.
5. *Theoretical knowledge.* Understanding of theoretical approaches to investigative reasoning and theories of crime.

6. *Management skills.* Skills to manage and control case information, implement investigative action, formulate investigative strategies, verify expert advice, prioritize lines of enquiry, formulate media strategies, awareness of resource availability and knowledge of roles of personnel available to the investigation. Manage knowledge and learning through the use of research skills to enable the detective to remain up to date.

7. *Investigative skills.* Interview techniques, presenting evidence, cultivating informants, extracting core information (from files, reports, victims and witnesses), file construction, appraising and evaluating information, ability to absorb and manage large volumes of information, statement taking, problem solving, formulating lines of enquiry, creating slow time, assimilating information from crime scene, continually reviewing lines of enquiry, questioning and challenging legal parties.

8. *Interpersonal skills.* Ability to communicate and establish a rapport with a range of people, remaining open minded, awareness of consequences of actions and avoidance of speculation.

Chapter 5
Corporate Compliance

Corporate compliance is important in a number of areas. For example, corporate compliance with international human rights standards is important, where employees have certain economic, social and cultural rights (Nolan and Taylor, 2009). In our perspective of white-collar crime and corporate reputation, corporate compliance with not only laws and regulations, but also norms and values in society is important.

Control and influence as two main approaches to combating white-collar crime are in line with findings made in a study by Bucy *et al.* (2008). The study indicates that there are four characteristics of organizations that discourage criminal activity. First, the corporation is not only driven by the bottom line. There is no overriding focus on profit and meeting numbers. Next, an effective corporate compliance plan prevents fraud and other kinds of white-collar crime. Third, effective internal control is assured with a strong and independent board, the presence of both internal and external auditors, appropriate checks and balances throughout the company, and a recentralized management structure. The final characteristic is whether an organization discourages crime in the corporate culture. When management sends the message that questionable behavior will not be tolerated, the corporate environment is less likely to be exposed to crime. While compliance planing and internal control have to do with controlling, bottom-line reluctance and corporate culture has to do with influencing.

Bucy *et al.* (2008) found that inside and outside corporate counsel and independent auditors play increasingly important roles in verifying ethical and legal compliance. The key to deterring and detecting white-collar crime is effective corporate compliance.

Compliance Officer

The compliance officer's responsibility is to ensure there are adequate internal procedures and processes to drive integrity and ethical conduct throughout the organization. The compliance officer's primary role is to prevent, detect and respond to unethical and/or unlawful behavior. The compliance officer is sometimes also titled ethics & compliance officer and responsible for regulatory compliance as well as ensuring high ethical standards by all employees. The roles and responsibilities of the compliance officer were primarily defined as part of the Sarbanes Oxley Act (SOX) of 2002. SOX drove the need for a more transparent corporate structure, and the compliance officer position was further developed into being responsible for having the right controls, education and reporting channels to increase transparency.

The compliance officer requires the highest ethical standard and is in many organizations an independent function with the responsibility to define the strategy according to risks for the company. Therefore, depending on the company and industry it is operating in, the compliance officer may report directly to the board of directors. In other companies the compliance officer will report directly to the chief executive officer, or the compliance officer may act as a function within the general counsel or report to the chief financial officer.

Among the responsibilities of the compliance officer in order to prevent violations, is the task to establish appropriate internal procedures. This may include regulatory compliance, i.e., ensuring that each function at each location is aware and complying with current regulatory requirements and knows how to deal with governments. It may include developing processes for how employees and third parties interact. International trade compliance is another significant area of responsibility that might be included. In addition, a company must have appropriate processes to deal with risks regarding improper payments, anti money laundering and other types of misconduct. The implementation of a company's compliance process can be completed by means of training all employees, and targeting particular functions for certain risk areas. Both live and electronic training may be used to increase awareness. Developing compliance processes is performed by assessing issues such as the organization's risks by the industry it is in, type of customers and suppliers, number of employees, and its geographical location.

In the event of compliance violations, the compliance officer's role is to ensure there are sufficient systems to detect these issues. This can be done through a compliance structure, creating reporting lines such as an ombudsman network, working with other functions such as legal and HR departments, and leveraging internal audit. Most important is the need to leverage all employees to raise awareness and concerns, and drive a culture of open reporting for transparency throughout the entire organization. Once a compliance concern has been detected, the compliance officer must ensure adequate processes are established to respond effectively and efficiently to the concern. There should be a process to categorize the concern and assign appropriate resources to clarify and potentially correct the concern if necessary.

Compliance Plan

The lack of a strong compliance plan leaves a company vulnerable to criminal activity. A strong compliance plan can ensure regulatory compliance through an internal system of checks and balances. In this perspective, Weismann (2009: 627) applied rational choice theory to study normative ethical corporate behaviors:

> Rational choice theory as a basis for predicting corporate behaviors in the marketplace from an institutional perspective relies on two key assumptions. First, corporations will achieve regulatory

compliance through an internal system of checks and balances, which can be relied upon by the regulators. Second, the least intrusion by regulators into internal corporate affairs provides the most efficient and effective means of corporate governance and internal control practices.

A compliance plan represents a form of social influence pressure. Obedience pressure is considered a special kind of social influence pressure, and there are two other types of social influence pressure: compliance pressure and conformity pressure (Baird and Zelin, 2009: 2):

> Compliance pressure is similar to obedience pressure, except that compliance pressure can come from one's peers as well as from superiors, while obedience pressure must come from an authority figure. Conformity pressure refers to pressure to conform to perceived or societal norms.

In the empirical study by Bucy *et al.* (2008), most participants stressed a well-implemented compliance and ethics program as most important to discourage and prevent white-collar crime. The key components of an effective compliance program are: an anonymous hotline for reporting suspect behavior, routine training for employees, proper oversight, and swift punishment of those involved in detected crime. The second most consistently cited corporate characteristic identified by participants was the corporate culture dictated by strong management. A true commitment to compliance and ethical conduct by upper management that permeates all levels of the company is a key in ensuring law-abiding behavior within an organization. In third place among participants came strong internal and external controls, and then finally supplementing bottom-line focus with integrity and accountability focus.

Gabel *et al.* (2009) argue that corporate compliance programs have never offered a complete defense to liability, but they have emerged to focus on the prevention of illegalities. As the business enterprise became increasingly important in society, self-regulation became more common within corporations and across industries.

Corporate compliance is required from corporate citizenship, where corporate citizenship describes the role of the corporation in administering citizenship rights for individuals and promoting socially responsible conduct. When doing so, corporations take on similar responsibilities as individual citizens. Good corporate citizens, like private persons, are expected to obey the law and contribute to the functioning of society.

Compliance Leadership

Bucy *et al.* (2008) also studied qualities of corporate leaders who encourage law-abiding behavior. A strong sense of personal integrity was the theme mentioned by most study participants when asked what characteristics chief executives should possess to encourage law-abiding behavior within a company. Integrity, honesty, and an intact moral compass are important qualities. A demonstrated commitment to community service and social concerns is an important quality as well.

The author of this book conducted a survey of white-collar crime in 2010. Many responses to open-ended questions from chief financial officers (CFOs) mentioned compliance:

"Raised the issue immediately with compliance leader and checked that it is followed through, perhaps also inform chairman of the board if lack of response"
"We have systems for reporting internally where we both can inform anonymously or with full name. In addition I would as a first step inform the compliance officer or CEO"
"Compliance officer will be informed"
"Inform corporate compliance executive who has the right to ask for direct access to the board"
"Banks have relatively strong oversight regime; external and internal auditors, finance authority, financial, compliance and risk controller, control committee, auditing committee and also money laundering responsible"
"Introduce compliance organization, introduce P2P processes and also an open and continuous communication around dangers that something can happen and educating what to do if something should happen"
"Compliance, ethics, whistle blowing possibility"

Forensic accounting as a discipline has its own models and methodologies of investigative procedures that search for assurance, attestation and advisory perspectives to produce legal evidence. It is concerned with the evidentiary nature of accounting data, and as a practical field, is concerned with accounting fraud and forensic auditing; compliance, due diligence, and risk assessment; detection of financial statement misrepresentation and financial statement fraud (Skousen and Wright, 2008); tax evasion; bankruptcy and valuation studies; violations of accounting regulations; non-standard entries, structured transactions, records tampering, and earnings mismanagement.

Hansen (2009) argues that prevention of corporate crime should not only be the concern of regulatory and law enforcement agencies. Corporations stand to lose more than reputation when financial scandals occur. Even when white-collar crime does not reach Royal Bank of Scotland, Enron or WorldCom proportions, corporations are damaged. It is estimated that white-collar crime can cost companies on average six percent of annual sales.

When enforcement leads to market loss and reputation cost, companies are more willing to internalize legal codes of conduct. Rational choice theory was applied here by Weismann (2009) to study compliance by business organizations. In the rational choice perspective, managerial decision making in bribe transactions or other kinds of white-collar crime is affected by perceived necessity of the crime and approval by white-collar management. Crime such as bribery is, however, perceived as a negative choice where managers focus on the unethical and non-compliance nature of the act.

Self Regulation

Gabel *et al.* (2009) studied whether corporate citizenship in the form of volunteerism may have positive consequences for legal compliance. Their study is one of the first attempts to empirically associate potentially unrelated aspects of a firm's corporate citizenship activities and obligations and to connect such behavior with legal decision making. They found a relationship between the extent of volunteering and compliance intentions for one compliance scenario, indicating some limited initial support for their contention that spirit-of-the-law ethical programs and letter-of-the-law compliance may be intertwined and should be considered in concert.

Weismann (2009) argues that the self-regulatory model of corporate governance in the global business environment has failed. The model rests on the theory of self-regulation as the most effective and efficient means to achieve corporate self-restraint in the marketplace. However, that model seems to fail in achieving regular compliance with basic ethical and legal behaviors as evidenced by a century of repeated corporate debacles. Some examples in the USA include Enron and WorldCom, some examples in the five million people state of Norway include Sponsor Service, Finance Credit, Municipality of Oslo, Ullevål University Hospital, Norwegian Red Cross, and Screen Communication. In other parts of Europe, we find Siemens (Germany), IT Factory (Denmark) and Glitnir Bank (Island).

The self-regulation model is premised on self-policing with regulatory oversight. A critical component of the model is that both external and internal oversight must be credible in terms of enforcement (Weismann, 2009: 625):

> A corollary of credible external oversight is enforcement. The importance of enforcement in the sphere of corporate governance cannot be minimized, particularly where self-policing fails. Enforcement reaffirms the value and importance of compliance.

Laws and regulations backed by credible enforcement create the basic expectation against which companies may benchmark legal behaviors and consequences of non-compliance.

Whistle Blowing

An important source of information in corporate compliance work is whistle blowing. For the future of whistle blowing in organizations, whistle blowing among young employees is of special interest. In a survey conducted by Stansbury and Victor (2009), they found that respondents who were both young and had short organizational tenure were substantially less likely than other respondents to report misconduct that they observed in the workplace to an authority. Based on this research result, they propose that the life-course model of deviance can help account for this attenuation of acquiescence in misbehavior. As employees learn to perceive informal pro-social control during their socialization into the workforce, it might be assumed that they will become more willing to blow the whistle on misconduct.

The Stansbury and Victor (2009) study revealed that young and short-tenured employees do perceive less informal pro-social control, and that informal pro-social control does boost whistle blowing. This is interesting to ethics and compliance officers as well as oversight agencies that are concerned about their ability to detect misbehavior that threatens the organization or its stakeholders. They may wish to devote efforts not only to formulate training that introduces new employees to the organization's standards and systems, but also to enhance new employees' social bonding with others.

While whistle blowing is found to be an important factor in bringing criminal police officers to justice, whistle blowing is a complicated issue both in theory and practice. For example, Varelius (2009) phrased the question: Is whistle blowing compatible with employee loyalty? Whistle blowing appears to involve a conflict between employee loyalty and protection of organizational and public interest. However, it might be argued that blowing the whistle about one's colleague's or employer's wrongdoing and being loyal to them serves the same goal, the moral good of the employer.

Varelius (2009) assessed this philosophical argument for the conclusion that the moral problem of whistle blowing is not real. He argues that being loyal to one's employer might be incompatible with blowing the whistle about wrongdoing, because employee loyalty and whistle blowing do not necessarily serve the same objective. He seems to argue against those who believe that loyalty and whistle blowing both see the moral good of the object. He seems to think that loyalty might still very well be a serious issue impeding whistle blowing, i.e., that whistle blowing might well be disloyal.

It has been argued that whistle blowing reveals most of the white-collar crime that is prosecuted in court. According to Pickett and Pickett (2002), policing financial crime is very much concerned with whistle blowing in addition to detection, roles of shareholders and main board, chief executives and senior executives, investigations, and forensics. As a source of suspicion and evidence, whistle blowers play an important role in detecting white-collar crime. However, as one of the respondents in our survey mentioned, it is important for a whistle blower to consider who should hear the whistle blowing:

> "Whistle blowing to the top is risky, since the receiver of the message may be involved in the crime"

Several respondents stressed the importance of whistle blowing routines by informing trustworthy people such as executives in charge of ethics or external auditors. Some respondents also stress the importance of protection of whistle blowers, as there has been a tendency by chief executives to go after the whistle blower if the whistle blowing was lacking hard evidence (Acquaah-Gaise, 2000: 19):

> Of course while encouraging whistle blowing we should not create an atmosphere where disgruntled employees find fertile ground to make unsubstantiated allegations against colleagues and superiors.

In 2003, whistle blowers in the USA received $4.1 million in rewards. This is what Tellechea (2008) calls reverse corruption, where individuals and entities are attracted to incentives to uncover and report misconduct by quickly and efficiently giving them a share of any seized funds.

Whistle blowing is an important function and whistle blowers are important persons in both private and public organizations to reveal misconduct by employees and executives. It has been argued that some organizations, such as police organizations, make it difficult to be a whistle blower because of the code of silence in some organizational cultures.

According to Johnson (2005), whistle blowing is a distinct form of dissent consisting of four elements: (1) the person acting must be a member or former member of the organization at issue; (2) his or her information must be about nontrivial wrongdoing in that organization; (3) he or she must intend to expose the wrongdoing, and (4) he or she must act in a way that makes the information public. According to Vadera *et al.* (2009) whistle blowing is the disclosure by organizational members (former or current) of illegal, immoral, or illegitimate practices under the control of their employers, to persons or organizations that may be able to effect action.

However, definitions of a whistle blowing act and a whistle blower vary. For example, a whistleblower may be defined as a person who alleged misconduct. The misconduct may be classified in many ways, for example, a violation of a law, a rule, regulation and/or a direct threat to public interest, such as fraud, health/safety violations, and corruption. The term "whistle blower" derives from the practice of English police constables, who would blow their whistles when they noticed the commission of a crime. The whistle would alert both law enforcement officers and the general public of danger. Today, most whistle blowers are internal whistle blowers that report misconduct to a fellow employee or superior within their company. Some whistle blowers turn to the public by telling their story to journalists from the mass media.

Whistle blowing does often still have consequences in terms of retaliation against the whistle blower. Retaliation examples are known from the press and from other research. For example, Bjørkelo *et al.* (2008) tell the story of retaliation and dismissal of a whistle blower in a Norwegian health organization. The whistle blower blew the whistle internally on unethical coercive treatment of patients. He then blew the whistle externally when the wrongdoing was not stopped. Retaliation followed and culminated with dismissal when the whistle blower refused to accept relocation to a job with no work assignments. He then sued his employer for unjust dismissal and lost in several judicial courts.

In a study of whistle blowing and the code of silence in police agencies, Rothwell and Baldwin (2006, 2007) identified predictors of police willingness to blow the whistle and police frequency of blowing the whistle on seven forms of misconduct. The results indicate that two variables, a policy mandating the reporting of misconduct and supervisory status, surface as the most consistent predictors of whistle blowing. Contrary to popular belief, the results also show that police are slightly less inclined than civilian public employees to subscribe to a code of silence.

Vadera *et al.* (2009) tried to find more explanations for what differentiates whistle blowers from those who observe a wrongdoing but chose not to report it. They identified the following explanations from other research studies:

➢ Federal whistle blowers were motivated by concern for public interest, were high performers, reported high levels of job security, job achievement, job commitment and job satisfaction, and worked in high-performing work groups and organizations.
➢ Anger at wrongful activities drove individuals to make internal reports to management. Retaliation by management shifted individuals' focus away from helping their organizations or victims and toward attaining retribution.

> Whistle blowing was more likely when observers of wrongdoing held professional positions, had more positive reactions to their work, had longer service, were recently recognized for good performance, were male, were members of larger work groups, and were employed by organizations perceived by others to be responsive to complaints.
> Whistle blowing was more frequent in the public sector than in the private.
> Whistle blowing was strongly related to situational variables with seriousness of the offense and supportiveness of the organizational climate being the strongest determinants.
> Inclination to report a peer for theft was associated with role responsibility, the interests of group members, and procedural perceptions.

It has been argued that whistle blowing is not common in special organizations such as the police. Most people in developed countries are familiar with whistle blowers — people who report corruption, fraud and abuse of in their own organizations. Some organizations make whistle blowing very difficult and thus less probable. Johnson (2005) found that the police department is one of these organizations.

She argues that the character of the police department not only makes whistle blowing less likely to occur; it ironically makes it even more necessary. In addition, she demonstrates that resistance from police departments and their retaliation against whistle blowers costs them and the public dearly. According to Porter and Warrender (2009), the prevalence of police deviance is a much-debated statistic and one that is often rife with problems.

Police officers who witness misconduct are often torn between their duty to reveal the truth and help stop criminal behavior, and group pressures to keep silent (Prenzler, 2009: 38):

> The latter pressures can be extremely intense, including ostracism, bullying, and even death threats.

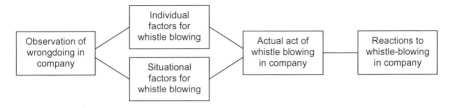

Figure 1.   Areas of Whistle Blowing Research.

In their review of the whistle blowing literature, Vadera *et al.* (2009) found that research in this field can largely be divided into studies examining the predictors of the observation of wrongdoing, the antecedents of the actual acts of whistle blowing, the process of whistle blowing, and the factors that predict retaliation against whistle blowers. Figure 1 offers an illustration of the whistle blowing research areas.

Whistle blowers can have a significant impact on corporations. When an employee notifies the public of wrongdoing within an organization, unwanted public scrutiny, regulatory action and litigation may arise.

The philosophical question raised by Varelius (2009) still remains, i.e., whether whistle blowing is compatible with employee loyalty. While employee loyalty is a concept without any criteria other than being loyal to whatever goes on in the organization, whistle blowing is a concept concerned with fighting bad things and encouraging good things. Loyalty does not need to seek the good of its object. The conception of loyalty that allows the moral problem of whistle blowing to arise does not require that the object of loyalty is morally acceptable. The notion of loyalty is concerned with faithful adherence to one's promise, oath, or word of honor. This notion of loyalty stresses adherence and allegiance to the object of loyalty, but it does not say that loyalty must seek the moral good of its object.

Compliance Levels

A system for evaluation of compliance levels has been developed according to recommendations by the Financial Action Task Force (FATF). The FATF was formed in 1989 by the G-7 group of countries, motivated by the General Assembly of the United Nations' adoption of a universal pledge to put a halt to money laundering, fuelled largely at that time by the laundering of illegal drug trade money. One of the FATF's first tasks was to develop measures to combat money laundering (Johnson, 2008).

A set of forty recommendations was issued by the FATF. They were designed to provide a comprehensive strategy for action against money laundering. FATF members have been evaluated over a number of years against these recommendations and more recently against the Nine Special Recommendations using self-assessment and/or mutual assessment procedures. Self-assessment is a questionnaire-based yearly exercise. Mutual evaluation involves an onsite visit by experts from other member countries in the areas of law, financial regulation, law enforcement, and international co-operation (Johnson, 2008).

The result of a mutual evaluation may be one of the following compliance levels (Johnson, 2008):

➢ Non-Compliant (NC). There are major shortcomings, with a large majority of the essential criteria not being met.
➢ Partially Compliant (PC). Some substantive action has been taken, and there is compliance with some of the essential criteria.
➢ Largely Compliant (LC). Only minor shortcomings, with a large majority of the essential criteria being fully met.
➢ Fully Compliant (FC). The recommendation is fully observed with respect to all essential criteria.

To be able to compare compliance across countries, each compliance level was assigned a numerical level: NC = 0, PC = 0.33, LC = 0.67

and FC = 1.0. The following countries achieved highest compliance scores (Johnson, 2008):

Belgium	0.77
UK	0.70
USA	0.69
Portugal	0.69
Norway	0.68
Switzerland	0.64
Ireland	0.63

Johnson (2008) argues that the results here should be used as a guide only to the ranking and compliance of countries rather than some exact measurement of compliance. This is because compliance levels are very broad, where substituting a single value for each compliance level provides only a crude measure of compliance for comparisons to be made. Only a future system based on artificial intelligence might provide an exact measure of compliance.

Chapter 6

Corporate Governance

An important element in stakeholder trust in a company and thus the level of corporate reputation is corporate governance. As argued by James and Seipel (2010), an important element of user confidence is the perceived strength of companies' corporate governance. They studied the effects of decreased user confidence on perceived internal audit fraud protection.

Financial Statements

The confidence of financial statement users in the reliability of financial reports is influencing the availability of capital for the company on capital markets. Such confidence is vital for individual companies to attract capital and keep capital costs low. A bad corporate reputation caused by lack of confidence in financial statements from the company will make it difficult and expensive to attract capital for investments and cash flow.

Confidence in financial statements is part of corporate reputation that is influenced by the quality of corporate governance, which in turn is dependent on the competence of internal auditors (James and Seipel, 2010: 1):

> Internal auditors play an important role in corporate governance due to their role in monitoring organizational risk and controls in the best interest of external stakeholders. Risks and controls monitored often include those over financial reporting. Internal

auditors also frequently take a leadership role in helping boards of directors set a proper "tone at the top".

The importance of internal audit to the actual and perceived quality of financial reporting and thus to the perception included in corporate reputation has been noted in several studies reviewed by James and Seipel (2010). Their own study examined the change in lender perceptions of the internal audit function over a time period characterized by several high-profile frauds such as Enron. Understanding these changes in user perceptions may help determine actions that can enhance public confidence and corporate reputation. Results show an overall drop in lenders' confidence in the ability and willingness of internal auditors to prevent fraudulent reporting.

Governance Systems

Corporate governance is the systems and structures through which companies are directed and run (Goldschmidt, 2004). Governance is a system and process by which an organization is to operate. Governance is an established and agreed structure in which the goals are to be met. The concept of governance deals with several normative principles including accountability, transparency, participation, responsiveness, equity, and the rule of law. The concept is based on an assumption that all organizations have the need to benchmark operations against governance standards (Jones, 2009).

Corporate governance has to do with the allocation of rights and obligations among the organization's stakeholders, including shareholders, managers, workers, and others with a stake in the corporation. Capron and Guillén (2009: 805) argue that national corporate governance institutions have a strong impact on the standards of governance in corporations:

> The rights and obligations of the various stakeholders are defined and enforced to varying degrees depending on the institutions of corporate governance present in a given country. Those institutions

include formal laws and regulations, codes of good governance, taken-for-granted assumptions about the appropriate role of the various stakeholders, and other informal norms of behaviour sanctioned by tradition or practice.

They view regulative institutions, including those associated with corporate governance, not just as constraints, but also as elements that support and empower actors. Institutions contribute to constituting actors as such and to preserving their roles, rights, and obligations over time.

An important goal of corporate governance is to reduce the risk of economic crime. In the perspective of agency theory, greed can lead agents and managers to theft, corruption, fraud and/or manipulation. They will steal from their principals if only they get the chance. Without corporate governance, principals tend to count on others to do what is necessary such as instructing and monitoring their agents.

For the purpose of linking corporate governance norms to economic crime, Nestor (2004) distinguished two types of economic crime that are likely to occur within a corporate setting:

➤ Economic crime that has a direct bearing on the way a corporation manages its resources and distributes economic returns among its different constituencies. These governance-related types of crime mainly have effect within the economic domain of a specific company. They include accounting fraud, insider trading and self-dealing.
➤ Economic crime that is perpetrated within a corporate framework but whose direct results are primarily felt outside the corporate sphere and are not as such of direct concern to governance design. However, it is of indirect concern to governance design, since the quality of corporate governance has an impact on the tendency of criminal options to corporate insiders. Bribery and corruption, money laundering, tax-related crimes and financing of terrorist organizations are among such types of crime.

While the first type is concerned with internal effects and internal victims, the second type is concerned with external effects and external victims. Nestor (2004) argued that the two types require different approaches to effective detection, effective prevention and liability. By narrowing liability to the actual perpetrators of economic crime, better corporate governance might improve the fight against corporate crime.

Executive Roles at Risk

While corporate governance is the systems and structures through which companies are directed and run, white-collar crime is misuse of the same systems and structures for personal and/or organizational gain. White-collar criminals are individuals who take part in the corporate governance by exercising power and influence in decision making and operations. Therefore, the assignment of roles in corporate governance must reflect and compensate for risks involved in executive roles exposed to white-collar crime.

In the survey research introduced earlier, the next set of questions in the Norwegian survey was concerned with positions most likely to get involved in white-collar crime. As listed in Table 1, a person with management position in the purchasing function is most likely to get involved in white-collar crime. On a scale from 1 (very unlikely) to 5 (very likely), a procurement manager had a likelihood score of 3.6.

The least likely position for white-collar crime is a person from external auditing. This is an interesting result, since Norman *et al.* (2010: 1) found that external auditors are subject to conflicts of interest:

> Research demonstrates that external auditors' conflicts of interest (e.g., legal requirements to be independent and provide unbiased evaluations of financial disclosures versus incentives to maintain fees and create employment opportunities with clients) influence external auditors' objectivity and independence.

Table 1.   Average Responses to Questions on Probability of White-Collar Crime by Different Internal and External Positions (1 - very unlikely, 5 - very likely)

Rank	Position	Probability
1	A person in procurement management	3.5
2	A person in marketing management	3.1
3	A person in executive management	3.0
4	A person in corporate middle management	3.0
5	A person in information technology management	2.8
6	An external consultant in business development	2.7
7	A person from public relations consulting	2.6
8	A person from external accounting firm	2.4
9	A person from the company board	2.4
10	A person from external law firms	2.2
11	A person from external auditing	1.9

There were 116 male CFOs and 24 female CFOs in the sample. Men considered the likelihood of white-collar crime to be higher than women for board, purchasing function, market function, auditing, law firm, and accounting firm. Women considered the likelihood of white-collar crime to be higher than men for top management, middle management, business consultant and media consultant. However, none of these differences were statistically significant.

Our statistical correlation analysis has so far concentrated on responses to statements about magnitude and attitude, and probability and consequence as dimensions of risk. Next, correlation analysis is applied to responses on the likelihood of persons in various trusted positions committing white-collar crime. Table 2 lists correlation coefficients.

In this table there are fewer significant correlations as compared to earlier correlation tables. The strongest correlation is found between an IT manager involved in crime and an external auditor involved in crime with a significant correlation coefficient of 0.722. If an external auditor is believed to be involved in crime, not only is the IT manager also believed to be involved in crime, but PR

Table 2. Correlations Between Responses to Vulnerability of Persons in Trusted Positions (statistical significance of .05 at* and .01 at**)

	PR Consultant	External Accountant	IT Manager	Marketing Manager	External Lawyer	Middle Manager	Procurement Manager	Business Consultant	Board Member	External Auditor
Top manager	−.112	.045	−.185	−.033	.494**	−.118	.440**	.004	−.050	.040
PR consultant		.195	.649**	.374**	−.005	.332*	.126	.008	.392**	.594**
External accountant			.211	.260	−.025	−.031	.137	.162	−.182	.022
IT manager				.203	−.132	.480**	−.037	.068	.361**	.722**
Marketing manager					.487**	.381**	.280*	.423**	.057	.246
External lawyer						.202	.463**	.280*	−.080	.130
Middle manager							.234	.201	.230	.695**
Procurement manager								.210	−.059	.298*
Business consultant									.114	.005
Board member										.438**

consultant, middle manager and board member as well. If a top manager is believed to be involved in white-collar crime, then an external lawyer and a purchasing manager is likely to be involved in such crime as well.

When exploratory factor analysis is applied to the different positions, the first factor includes the following positions:

> A person from public relations consulting
> A person in information technology management
> A person in marketing management
> A person in corporate middle management
> A person from external auditing

This list comprises a group of positions that have a profession as their basis, apart from middle managers. Public relations, information technology, marketing and auditing all represent different professional disciplines. Based on such a theoretical understanding, it is possible to define these positions as a multiple item scale. When computing the reliability of this scale, an acceptable reliability in terms of Cronbachs alpha of 0.810 is achieved (Hair *et al.*, 2010).

Lack of knowledge on white-collar crime can result in not recognizing it in own professions and type of businesses. That can be the reason for stating it to be more common in other industries and in the public sector more than private sector. This is in accordance to the third main perception, namely their interpretation of risk. Larger risk of misconduct is believed to happen among chief executives. They also believe that mostly, financial crime is something internal, and thus, do not recognize the risk in relation to external suppliers or for instance, accountants. The fourth perception, knowledge about offenders, is related to some general patterns. They believe that there is more white-collar crime in the public sector. They also find that employees within procurement are more at risk of white-collar crime, followed by employees working within marketing and executive personnel. This understanding can be related to easier access and the possibility of committing financial crime. These employees are in trusting positions with a large degree of responsibility, authority and power over financial dispositions. But they are also in positions where awareness of possible misconduct is probably more in focus. That is probably why executives' perception is that business corporations are generally competent at combating white-collar crime.

Stakeholder theory is a managerial conception of organizational strategy and ethics. The central idea is that an organization's success is dependent on how well it manages its relationships with key groups such as customers, employees, suppliers, communities, financiers, and others that can affect the realization of its purpose. The manager's job is to keep the support of all these groups, balancing their interests, while making the organization a place where stakeholder interests can be maximized over time (Freeman and Phillips, 2002). Upholding four principles (1) honoring agreements, (2) avoiding lying, (3) respecting the autonomy of others, and (4) avoiding harm to others, are a necessary precondition for efficient working. And thus, stakeholder theories of the firm establish economic relationships within a general context of moral management. Neglecting these dimensions, firms will have less satisfied stakeholders, and will show financial performance that is consistently below industry average (Shankman, 1999). Although white-collar crime is not very widespread, its consequence might be huge.

Some positions can be vulnerable to crime because of incentives like stock options and bonuses. Salary incentives can provide an incentive to engage in white-collar crime such as tax fraud and accounting malpractice (Bucy *et al.*, 2008).

Governance Principles

At the most basic level, a corporate governance problem arises whenever an outside investor wishes to exercise control differently from the executives of a business organization. According to

Becht *et al.* (2007: 833), most research on corporate governance has been concerned with the resolution of this collective action problem:

> The favoured mechanism for resolving collective action problems among shareholders in most countries appears to be partial ownership and control concentration in the hands of large shareholders. Two important costs of this form of governance have been emphasized: (i) the potential collusion of large shareholders with management against smaller investors and, (ii) the reduced liquidity of secondary markets. In an attempt to boost stock market liquidity and limit the potential abuse of minority shareholders some countries' corporate law drastically curbs the power of large shareholders.

Jones (2009) suggests a number of principles of modern governance:

➤ *Legitimacy*. The traditional organization is a hierarchically structured apparatus of command and control. Restructuring allows for greater participation and consensus among the actors within the organization. This idea reinforces a bottom-up process by recognizing that key buy-in is crucial to the development and actualization of change in the organization and the manner in which the organization carries out its primary mission.

➤ *Accountability*. Representative associations are encouraged in organizations, since the presence and ability to participate in such representative organizations by employees presents an air of organizational accountability. The ability to partake in representative organizations aids in building a consensus-based approach within organizations where employees have the ability to freely access information and are satisfied with their position within the information flow.

➤ *Performance*. The organization is more responsive, efficient, and effective under the governance paradigm. Efficiency and effectiveness are important because they aid in the mitigation of role ambiguity in a given task environment, and therefore act as a mechanism of control over discretion.

➤ *Fairness.* Equity and the rule of law are vital aspects to the promotion and perception of fairness. For democracy to be fostered inside the organization and subsequently transferred to the community, all persons working in the organization as well as those served by it must have the opportunity to receive the level of service desired. Taking an open systems approach, organizations exist to aid people.

Omoyele (2008) studied corporate governance as a contraption of the Financial Services Authority's accountability in the UK. He argues that the Financial Services Authority (FSA) should be responsible for the Combined Code on corporate governance. He argues in favor of obliging the FSA to adopt the Code as a way of making it accountable. The Combined Code on corporate governance is divided into two main sections. The first relates to companies and the other to institutional shareholders.

Spitzeck (2009) argues that corporations will not act responsibly as long as corporate social responsibility issues are not integrated in their decision-making and governance structures. He found that there is increasing CEO leadership for the corporate responsibility agenda of the firm. He also found that governance structures developed over time are now increasingly making use of corporate responsibility committees, and that firms with a corporate responsibility committee in place outperform others in the corporate responsibility indices.

Leader Types at Risk

As argued by Spitzeck (2009), corporations and hence executives will not act responsibly as long as corporate social responsibility issues are not integrated in their decision-making and governance structures. Such integration starts by eliminating rotten apples and replacing rotten barrels. Rotten apples have to be removed from the corporate governance structure, and a governance structure supporting rotten apples has to be renewed.

Governance structures have to reflect that a person in procurement management is much more likely to commit white-collar crime as compared to a person from the company board. Therefore, procurement management needs the tightest and most transparent governance structure.

There was an open-ended question in the questionnaire concerned with executive positions and leader types vulnerable to white-collar crime. The question was formulated like this: *What position categories and leader types are in your opinion most attracted to commit white-collar crime?*

Here are some of the responses to position categories:

> "Management and trusted persons, purchasers and those who sign contracts"
> "Top management and persons with access to and control over assets"
> "Brokers and banks, i.e., finance acrobats"
> "Managers who have the authority to commit the company financially"
> "Top executives who manipulate accounting to achieve extra bonus"
> "Leaders at the top who would like the company to avoid paying taxes"
> "Persons with close relationships to vendors and customers who handle large contracts"
> "Ambitious top executives who are exposed to great pressure and potential income by success"

Here are some of the responses to leader types:

> "Leader types with low integrity and moral"
> "Persons who are independent and without perception of values"
> "Individuals for personal gain or subject to pressure"
> "Leadership types who are dominating and authoritarian, whose subordinates do not dare to oppose"
> "Persons who have been in the business for a long time, who have a wide network, but have little hope to make progress in their careers and are dissatisfied with their current condition"
> "Those with a big ego, who implement military commando practices and do not accept critical questions"
> "Persons with a disorganized and messy private financial household"
> "Chief executives who have established good relationships over time with key employees by providing them favors so that they become part of the 'team' without really knowing it"

"Those charismatic ones who are dependent on success and who are assigned to make 'great' decisions on behalf of the corporation"

For executive positions, most respondents wrote text indicating procurement management, marketing management, and top management. Therefore, respondents confirmed the top of the list in Table 1. For leader types, a number of characteristics were mentioned, including: low integrity, no morals, dominating, authoritarian, dissatisfied, big ego, private financial problems, charismatic, and no ethics.

In an empirical study of white-collar crime by Bucy *et al.* (2008), they found that typical white-collar criminals might be characterized as personalities who are intelligent, arrogant, cunning, successful, greedy, willing to take risks, aggressive, narcissistic, determined and charismatic. This is in line with eight personality characteristics that fuel white-collar criminal activity: (1) need for control; (2) bullying; (3) charisma; (4) fear of failing; (5) company ambition; (6) lack of integrity; (7) narcissism; and (8) lack of social conscience.

Self-Regulation Governance

Hughes *et al.* (2008: 115) argue that much of the national media in the US has paid attention to corporate scandals where "know-nothing" CEOs and complacent/conflicted auditors missed the accounting frauds:

> In each case, "revelations" abound about lax corporate control environments and defective or non-existent audit procedures that prevented identification of potential abuses.

This chapter is concerned with the following research question: *How will the chief financial officer (CFO) prevent white-collar crime in his or her business organization?* Results from a survey of CFOs in Norway are applied to answer this research question.

The open-ended question in the questionnaire to the CFO about prevention of white-collar crime was formulated as: *How can white-collar crime best be prevented in your company?*

Responses were classified by applying content analysis (Riffe and Freitag, 1997). In the first round of text reading, potential topics were identified.

Two main topics were identified. The first group of responses is concerned with the ability to control by means of efficient and effective control routines, transparent guidelines, reactions and consequences for offences and misconduct. This main topic is labeled the reactive strategy in prevention of white-collar crime.

The other group of responses is concerned with the ability to influence by means of values and ethics, recruitment and hiring processes, attitudes of integrity and accountability, and visible and determined leadership. This other main topic is labeled the proactive strategy in prevention of white-crime.

Based on the discussion of self-regulation in prevention of white-collar crime, we conceptualize self-regulation as consisting of both the reactive as well as the proactive strategy. Thus, self-regulation consists of control and influence as illustrated in Figure 1.

As mentioned, the open-ended question in the questionnaire to the CFO about prevention of white-collar crime was formulated as: *How can white-collar crime best be prevented in your company?* Examples of control statements provided by respondents include:

> *"Good internal control"*
> *"Banks have a relatively strong regulation regime, external and internal auditor, finance authorities, compliance and risk controllers, control committee, auditing group and money laundering regulation"*
> *"Good control routines and internal procedures"*
> *"Access control and reliable approval procedures"*
> *"Control routines with division of responsibilities"*

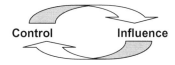

Figure 1.   Self-Regulation in Companies for Prevention of White-Collar Crime.

"Efficient systems and routines, regular internal controls"
"Implement effective control systems"

Examples of influence statements provided by respondents include:

"Continuous work on culture - values - ethics, show zero tolerance in relation to misconduct"
"Openness with contacts and financial information"
"Attitudes of honesty and accountability as a culture in the company at all levels"
"An explicit and visible leadership that monitors the organization"
"Good hiring procedures"
"Focus on ethics, where management is a good example in all situations"
"Build common culture, behavior, set of values and company identity"

Among the initial responses of 47 completed questionnaires for this question, the following distribution was identified:

➢ *Control.* 25 out of 47 respondents would focus on controlling and auditing, thus 53% for control.
➢ *Influence.* 22 out of 47 respondents would focus on influencing and behavior, thus 47% for influence.

This is an interesting result as there is almost an even distribution between the two main themes in Figure 1, where half of the respondents emphasize control, while the other half emphasizes influence.

After a reminder was mailed to non-respondents, a total of 47 completed questionnaires were received, which is exactly the same number as in the first round. The distribution among chief financial officers in terms of responses to the open-ended question was as follows:

➢ *Control.* 20 out of 47 respondents would focus on controlling and auditing, thus 43% for control.
➢ *Influence.* 27 out of 47 respondents would focus on influencing and behavior, thus 57% for influence.

Influencing and Controlling

We find an even distribution among control and influence, but the majority in this second round emphasizes influence to prevent white-collar crime. In total, the following distribution for all 94 respondents that filled in this open-ended question was as follows:

> ➢ *Control.* 45 out of 94 respondents would focus on controlling and auditing, thus 48% for control.
> ➢ *Influence.* 49 out of 94 respondents would focus on influencing and behavior, thus 52% for influence.

In terms of self-regulation, respondents who emphasize influence are slightly more in number than respondents who emphasize control. Few respondents seem to emphasize the need to analyze risks before deciding to control or influence. Most responses are formulated in a way that indicates a victim perspective rather than an offender perspective.

After the second and final mailing of reminders, 17 more responses to this question were obtained, where 9 emphasized control and 8 emphasized influence. Therefore, we have in total the following results:

1. *Influencing.* This is a proactive measure. 57 out of 111 respondents would focus on influencing and behavior, thus 51% were in favor of influence. Influencing might be to demonstrate a behavior in top management that considers ethics before running for short-term profits, to have open processes and dialogues internally and externally with vendors and customers, to establish corporate values of openness and trust, to initiate awareness campaigns for all employees, to demonstrate zero tolerance towards white-collar crime, to build actions on solid knowledge, and to practice transparent empowerment.
2. *Controlling.* This is a reactive measure. 54 out of 111 respondents would focus on controlling and auditing, thus 49% were in favor of control. Controlling might be to continuously improve internal

control routines, to implement strong authorization procedures, to practice segregation of duties, to adhere to the 4-eyes principle in approval of invoices and payments, to perform audit on both regular and irregular basis, to introduce complaints to the organization, to divide work into processes and sub-processes including control, to implement policies for behavior and consequences for misconduct, to frequently update passwords and access rights, and to develop control expertise.

Responsible Business

Responsible business attitudes and practices have been the focus of attention of much recent research (Avram and Kühne, 2008; Courrent and Gundolf, 2009; Hammann *et al.*, 2009; Moore *et al.*, 2009; Wilburn, 2009).

Avram and Kühne (2008) argue that stressing the notion that responsible business behavior is not a matter of getting companies to move away from their usual way of doing business. Rather, responsible business behavior constitutes the consciousness that a company can do well in the long run by paying attention to the environment and the society in which it operates. Many of the pressing social and environmental problems are caused and can be solved by companies.

Courrent and Gundolf (2009) studied managers' perception of their relationship to their environment on the nature of their ethics. They found significant statistical relationships between the variables that indicated perceived closeness to the community and ethical variables measuring corporate social responsibility.

Hammann *et al.* (2009) found that socially responsible management practices towards employees, customers and to a lesser extent, society, have a positive impact on the firm and its performance. Various types of socially responsible management practices with respect to these interest groups may enhance the competitive strengths of the enterprise and make good business sense.

Moore *et al.* (2009) developed a set of 16 criteria, divided into four groupings, for responsible business practice. The groups are labeled "governance", "employees", "stakeholders", and "external reporting". The "employee" group includes staff handbook, training for employees, and responsibility towards employees.

Wilburn (2009) suggests that businesses that want to be socially responsible, but do not have the resources of multinational corporations, can partner with non-governmental organizations (NGOs), not-for-profit organizations (NFPs), and religious organizations to access information about the culture, customs, and needs of the people in areas where they wish to do business. Without such information and knowledge, social responsibility initiatives by the corporation can have unintended consequences that are not beneficial to the community.

Limits to Responsibility

There are limits to corporate responsibility. For example, public sector capabilities are the responsibility of the government rather than the industry. However, in some less developed regions and countries, companies do tend to invest in public sector capabilities. The motivation can be to protect the present value of their investments in areas such as large-scale natural resource projects and to prevent or minimize any hostile actions by host governments and communities. Corporate initiatives may extend beyond national boundaries to create transparency (Crowson, 2009).

When corporate responsibility extends to public sector capabilities, then a bridge is created between business and societies representing values such as cooperation and collaboration. Waddock and McIntosh (2009) stress the importance of such a bridge through new approaches to leadership. They argue that a number of issues are no longer relevant either for business or society. Rather, an increasing number of issues are global in scale and require cooperation and collaboration rather than division of tasks and responsibilities.

Corporate responsibility certainly extends beyond the "do no harm" paradigm. Wettstein (2010) argues that there is a shift from negative to positive obligations. Powerful as they have become, large global companies can no longer merely make do with not doing any harm. They are expected to engage proactively in finding and implementing viable solutions for prevailing global problems such as climate change and transnational crime. Positive obligation implies new political responsibilities of multinational corporations even beyond the particular duty to promote just institutions.

Chapter 7

Stages of Corporate Responsibility

In this chapter, we suggest that the powerful concept of stages of growth is extremely important in management research. To capture this concept, we introduce stages of growth modeling and present elements of a growth stage theory exemplified with the case of corporate social responsibility (CSR). We propose that a CSR arrangement may change over time as the relationship between stakeholders matures. The changes occur in terms of discrete stages with their own unique characteristics.

Researchers have struggled for decades to develop stages of growth models that are both theoretically founded and empirically validated (e.g., Nolan, 1979; King and Teo, 1997). However, stages of growth models have the potential of creating new knowledge and insights into organizational phenomena. Such models represent theory-building tools that conceptualize evolution over time in a variety of areas. For researchers, a stage model represents a theory to be explored and empirically validated. For practitioners, a stage model represents a picture of evolution, where the current stage can be understood in terms of history and future.

Theory Building in Management Research

There are numerous examples of theory building in the management literature. An example found in the Academy of Management Review is the theory of psychological ownership in organizations by Pierce *et al.* (2001). They suggest that the powerful concept of "mine" is extremely important in organizations, as it is in other realms of human life. To capture this concept, they introduced the psychological ownership construct and presented elements of a theory of psychological ownership in organizations. According to their theory, organizational members may experience feelings of ownership for the organization or various organizational factors.

Another example of theory building is the theory of virtual customer environments developed by Nambisan (2002). A conceptual model of customer roles is an important part of the theory. The theory sets a broad agenda for future research that involves using a wide theoretical canvas to depict the underpinning design and deployment issues of virtual customer environments exemplified with the case of new product development.

A third and final example is the theory of corporate integrity developed by Maak (2008). The theory consists of a framework linking commitment, conduct, content, context, consistency, coherence, and continuity to explain integrity. These 7 C's of corporate integrity are explained in terms of their impact on our understanding of corporate social responsibility.

These four theories demonstrate the importance of and diversity in theory building and testing. These four examples also illustrate the challenges in theory building discussed by scholars such as DiMaggio (1995), Sutton and Staw (1995), and Weick (1995) more than a decade ago.

The academic debate started with Sutton and Staw (1995), who argued that references, data, variables, diagrams, and hypotheses are not theories. DiMaggio (1995) commented on Sutton and Staw by arguing that there are at least three views of what a theory should be: (1) theory as covering laws, (2) theory as enlightenment, and (3) theory as narrative.

Weick (1995) argued that the process of theorizing consists of activities like abstracting, generalizing, relating, selecting, explaining, synthesizing, and idealizing. These ongoing products summarize progress, give direction, and serve as place makers. It is in this sense of theorizing as suggested by Weick (1995) that we develop our stages of growth theory in this article.

A theory might be a prediction or explanation, a set of inter-related constructs, definitions, and propositions that presents a systematic view of phenomena by specifying relations among variables, with the purpose of explaining natural phenomena. The systematic view might be an argument, a discussion, or a rationale, and it helps to explain or predict phenomena that occur in the world. Some define theory in terms of relationships between independent and dependent variables, where theory is a collection of assertions, both verbal and symbolic, that identifies what variables are important and for what reasons, and that specifies how they are interrelated and why. It identifies the conditions under which variables should be related or not related. Other scholars have defined theory in terms of narratives and accounts (Colquitt and Zapata-Phelan, 2007).

It is difficult to overstate the importance of theory to management understanding of CSR issues. Theory allows analysts to understand and predict outcomes on a probabilistic basis (Colquitt and Zapata-Phelan, 2007). Theory allows analysts to describe and explain a process or sequence of events. Theory prevents analysts from being confused by the complexity of the real world by providing a linguistic tool for organizing a coherent understanding of the real world. Theory acts as an educational device that creates insights into intra-organizational as well as inter-organizational phenomena such as CSR functions.

Stage Modeling in Management Research

Stages of growth models have been used widely in both organizational research and information technology management research. According to King and Teo (1997), these models describe a wide variety of phenomena — the organizational life cycle, product life cycle, biological growth, and so forth. These models assume that predictable patterns (conceptualized in terms of stages) exist in the growth of organizations, the sales levels of products, the diffusion of information technology, and the growth of living organisms. These stages are (i) sequential in nature, (ii) occur as a hierarchical progression that is not easily reversed, and (iii) involve a broad range of organizational activities and structures.

Benchmark variables are often used to indicate characteristics at each stage of growth. A one-dimensional continuum is established for each benchmark variable. The measurement of benchmark variables can be carried out using Guttman scales (Nunnally and Bernstein, 1994; Frankfort-Nachmias and Nachmias, 2002). Guttman scaling is a cumulative scaling technique based on ordering theory that suggests a linear relationship between the elements of a domain and the items on a test.

Embodying such characteristics, organizational learning and innovation diffusion theory can be applied to explain stages of growth models. Organizational learning is sometimes placed at the center of innovation diffusion theory through a focus on institutional mechanisms that lower the burden of organizational learning related to IT adoption. Organizations may be viewed, at any given moment, as possessing some bundle of competence related to their current operational and managerial processes. In order to successfully assimilate a new process technology, an organization must somehow reach a state where its bundle of competence encompasses those needed to use the new technology (Fichman and Kemerer, 1997).

Innovations through stages of growth can be understood in terms of technology acceptance over time. Technology acceptance has been studied for several decades in information systems research. Technology acceptance models explain perceived usefulness and usage intentions in terms of social influence and cognitive instrumental processes. For example, Venkatesh and Davis (2000) found that social influence processes (subjective norm, voluntary, and image) and cognitive instrumental processes (job relevance, output quality, result demonstrability, and perceived ease of use) significantly influenced user acceptance. Similarly, Venkatesh (2000) identified determinants of perceived ease of use, a key driver of technology acceptance, adoption, and usage behavior.

Theory Building for Stage Models

Researchers have struggled for decades to develop stages of growth models that are both theoretically founded and empirically validated. Two decades ago, Kazanjian and Drazin (1989) found that the concept of stages of growth was already widely employed. Later, a number of multistage models have been proposed which assume that predictable patterns exist in the growth of organizations, and that these patterns unfold as discrete time periods best thought of as stages. These models have different distinguishing characteristics. Stages can be driven by the search for new growth opportunities or as a response to internal crises. Some models suggest that an organization progresses through stages while others argue that there may be multiple paths through the stages. Therefore, a stages of growth theory needs to allow for multiple paths through stages as long as they follow a unidirectional pattern.

Kazanjian and Drazin (1989) argued that either implicitly or explicitly, all stages of growth models share a common underlying logic. Organizations undergo transformations in their design characteristics, which enable them to face the new tasks or problems that growth elicits. The problems, tasks or environments may differ from model to model, but almost all suggest that stages emerge in a well-defined sequence, so that the solution of one set of problems or tasks leads to the emergence of a new set of problems or tasks that the organization must address. Growth in areas such as CSR maturity can be viewed as a series of evolutions and revolutions precipitated by internal crises related to leadership, control and coordination. The striking characteristic of this view is that the resolution of each crisis sows the seeds for the next crisis. Another view is to consider stages of growth as responses to the firm's search for new growth opportunities once prior strategies have been exhausted.

Benchmark variables in stages of growth models indicate the theoretical characteristics in each stage of growth. The problem with this approach is that not all indicators of a stage may be present in an organization, making it difficult to place the organization in any specific stage. Nevertheless, a stages of growth theory needs to allow for benchmark variables to be applied in the modeling process.

Guttman scaling is relevant and applicable to stages of growth modeling. Guttman scaling is also known as cumulative scaling or scalogram analysis. Guttman scaling is based on ordering theory that suggests a linear relationship between the elements of a domain and the items on a test. The purpose of Guttman scaling is to establish a one-dimensional continuum for a concept to measure. We would like a set of items or statements so that a respondent who agrees with any specific question in the list will also agree with all previous questions. This is the ideal for a stage model — or for any progression. By this we mean that it is useful when one progresses from one state to another, so that upon reaching the higher stage one has retained all the features of the earlier stage (Trochim, 2006). Therefore, a stages of growth theory might be empirically validated using variables that are measured on Guttman scales.

Based on the reviewed literature, four core topics emerge when theorizing stages of growth modeling:

➤ *Number of Stages.* Typically, stage models for empirical testing have four to eight stages. More importantly, the classification and identification of stages have to satisfy several criteria. First, all stages have to be conceptualized and theoretically defined as significantly different from each other. Second, no overlap in contents should be found between stages. Third, no stage should be perceived as a subcategory of another stage. Finally, each stage must be transferable to an empirical setting. These criteria determine which and how many stages are appropriate for a specific stage model.

➢ *Dominant Problems*. At each stage, a set of dominant problems is to be identified. Dominant problems imply that there is a pattern of primary concerns that organizations face for each theorized stage. In the area of CSR maturity, dominant problems can shift from lack of skills to lack of resources to lack of strategy associated with different stages of growth. How dominant problems change from one stage to another stage has to be conceptualized as well.

➢ *Benchmark Variables*. Benchmark variables in stages of growth models indicate the theoretical characteristics in each stage of growth. While dominant problems change from stage to stage, benchmark variables do not change. Only the attributes of benchmark variables change from stage to stage. For example, the role of management might be a benchmark variable, where the attributes change from entrepreneur via resource allocator to spokesman.

➢ *Paths of Evolution*. The most obvious path is from the initial stage via intermediary stages to the final stage. However, other paths are possible. For example, some stages may be bypassed and skipped. Also, a temporary return to an earlier stage might be possible as well.

Based on these four topics in theorizing stages of growth, four corresponding research propositions can be formulated as the core of a stage of growth theory:

Proposition 1. Organizational phenomena undergo transformations in their design characteristics that can be defined in terms of discrete stages of growth.

Proposition 2. Dominant problems at each stage of growth will statistically correspond with the conceptual formulations given for that stage.

Proposition 3. Values of benchmark variables for each stage of growth will statistically correspond with the conceptual formulations given for that stage.

Proposition 4: An organizational phenomenon shows a predictable pattern of development from first stage to second stage, and so on, until it reaches the final stage, either directly or via bypassed or revisited stages.

Modeling Process for Stage Models

Based on the suggested theory of stages of growth, a modeling process for stage models can be suggested. The modeling process needs to include all aspects identified in the research propositions. The modeling process is illustrated in Figure 1 and represents a theoretical as well as empirical research procedure where the object changes its status from a suggested stage model, via a conceptual and theoretical stage model, to an empirical stage model, and finally to a revised stage model:

> *Suggested Stage Model.* The initial stage model is based on ideas from both research and practice. Research literature has defined evolutionary aspects of the phenomenon, and practitioners perceive different maturity levels for the phenomenon.
> *Conceptual Stage Model.* The number of stages and the contents of stages are developed in an iterative cycle involving dominant

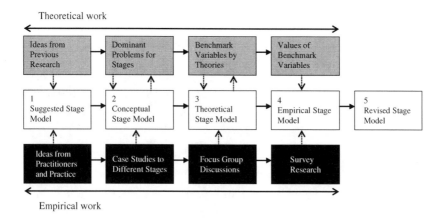

Figure 1.   Suggested Procedure for the Stages of Growth Modeling Process.

problems that seem different at various stages. Case studies are applied to illustrate content characteristics of each stage as well as significant differences between stages, where preceding and following stages have different kinds of dominant problems.

➢ *Theoretical Stage Model.* Relevant theories are applied to explain stages, their contents as well as the evolution from one stage to the next stage. Benchmark variables are derived from these theories. At the same time, theories and benchmark variables are discussed in focus groups.

➢ *Empirical Stage Model.* Each benchmark variable is assigned a benchmark value for each stage of growth. A survey is carried out, where stages, evolution as well as benchmark values are empirically tested.

➢ *Revised Stage Model.* Based on the empirical test from survey research, the empirical stage model is revised.

Corporate Social Responsibility

Corporate social responsibility is a concept related to the behaviour and conduct of corporations and those who are associated with them. During the best of times, it is a concept adopted and taken for granted. During the worst of times, however, corporate social responsibility becomes a threatening concept to most business as well as public organizations (Jayasuriya, 2006). Corporate social responsibility (CSR) is a set of voluntary corporate actions designed to improve corporate actions. These corporate actions not required by the law attempt to further some social good and extend beyond the explicit transactional interests of the firm. The voluntary nature of CSR means that these activities can be viewed as gifts or grants from the corporation to various stakeholder groups (Godfrey *et al.*, 2009).

Basu and Palazzo (2008) define corporate social responsibility as the process by which managers within an organization think about and discuss relationships with stakeholders as well as their roles in relation to the common good, along with their behavioral disposition with respect to the fulfillment and achievement of these roles and relationships. It is an intrinsic part of an organization's character, with the potential to discriminate it from other organizations that might adopt different types of processes.

Corporate social responsibility is a concept by which business enterprises integrate the principles of social and environmental responsibility in their operations as well as in the way they interact with their stakeholders. This definition shows two perspectives. First, social and environmental responsibility in their operations requires internal change processes to integrate the principles into business operations. Second, interactions with stakeholders require stakeholder engagement (Zollo *et al.*, 2009).

The concept of corporate social responsibility developed as a reaction against the classical and neo-classical recommendations from economics, where rational decision making and free markets are concentrated solely on profits. This narrow economic view has been questioned due to inconsistencies with the economic model and the evidence of unethical business practices. These problems have led to the realization that organizations should also be accountable for the social and environmental consequences of their activities (Mostovicz *et al.*, 2009).

Frontiers of Corporate Responsibility

According to Jayasuriya (2006), the frontiers of corporate responsibility continue to expand, casting a wider net to encompass almost all those who have something to do with corporate practices and management. Therefore, the regulatory landscape is rapidly changing and trained staff in corporations are required to deal with the new requirements. Staff training and supervision are major undertakings to improve the ability to carry out tasks involved in corporate social responsibility.

At the core of corporate social responsibility is the idea that it reflects the social imperatives and the social consequences of business success. It consists of clearly articulated and communicated policies and practices of corporations that reflect business responsibility for some of the wider societal good. It is differentiated from business fulfillment of core profit-making responsibility and from the social responsibilities of the government and public authorities (Matten and Moon, 2008).

Matten and Moon (2008) make a distinction between explicit and implicit corporate social responsibility. First, explicit responsibility describes corporate activities that assume responsibility for the interests of society, while implicit responsibility describes corporate role within the wider institutions in society. Next, explicit responsibility consists of voluntary corporate policies, while implicit responsibility consists of values and norms. Finally, explicit responsibility involves incentives and opportunities motivated by expectations, while implicit responsibility is motivated by societal consensus.

Sometimes employees may know of inappropriate conduct in the corporation but be unwilling to report it to the appropriate quarters for fear of reprisals. In a culture of communal responsibility for the efficient running of a company, all will consider it their proper duty and in their interest to expose wrongdoings at work (Acquaah-Gaisie, 2000: 19):

> If employees see that when they contribute to workplace integrity they advance their own wellbeing as well as that of the community they may be more willing to report suspicious conduct. Of course while encouraging whistle blowing we should not create an atmosphere where disgruntled employees find fertile ground to make unsubstantiated allegations against colleagues and superiors.

However, in other corporate cultures, deviant purposes can be chosen when a business corporation is trapped within doubtful, immoral or disloyal means that are used by competitors. Very often, organizational culture makes it possible to adopt organizational purposes or objectives, which are basically deviant in comparison with social norms, but in line with industry practices. Therefore, a business enterprise can be trapped by the business milieu as a social institution. They can be trapped by their own sector-based morality, which is oriented towards profit maximization where most or all means seem to be allowed. Dion (2009) suggests that globalization is indirectly making business corporations more deviant and reluctant to any external control, both because of the increasing oligopolization and because enterprises are searching for more freedom.

It can be argued that size, responsibility and hierarchical structure of large business corporations sometimes foster conditions that are conductive to organizational deviance and financial crime. In many situations of economic instability and crisis, the nature of organizational goals may promote illegal behaviour. Organizational goals can easily be perceived as absolute requirements with personal consequences following non-achievement. Therefore, goals may seem to justify almost any means used to fulfill goals (Dion, 2008).

Abuse of responsibility, rather than corporate social responsibility, may occur when the type of structure allows the company to decouple components if that is deemed necessary. Rules may be violated, decisions not implemented and inspection systems subverted or rendered so vague as to provide little coordination (Dion, 2008).

Corporate social responsibility has not been equally addressed in every country around the globe. Hansen (2009) argues that American corporations so far have been leading the trend towards increased awareness, with corporations in some other parts of the world just entering the debate.

Godfrey *et al.* (2009) phrased the question: Do shareholders gain when managers disperse corporate resources through activities classified as corporate social responsibility? Strategy scholars have recently developed a theoretical model that links such activities to shareholder value when a firm suffers a negative event. The insurance-like property of corporate social responsibility can be tested. Such activity can lead to positive attributions from stakeholders, who then temper their negative judgments and sanctions towards firms because of this goodwill.

Godfrey *et al.* (2009: 425) extended the risk management model by theorizing that some types of responsibility actions will be more likely to create goodwill and offer insurance-like protection and found a positive answer to the above question:

> We find that participation in institutional CSR activities — those aimed at a firm's secondary stakeholders or society at large — provides 'insurance-like' benefit, while participation in technical CSRs — those activities targeting a firm's trading partners — yields no such benefits.

The frontiers of corporate social responsibility are moving into a focus on a new relationship between business and society. That is, according to Waddock and McIntosh (2009), new ways of looking at the corporation and its role in society, both in practice and in management education. Management education, which has been criticized in the financial crisis period, has an important role to play, but in a changed form. Corporate responsibility is becoming a social movement.

Internal Change Management

There seems to be two perspectives on corporate social responsibility in terms of alignment between executive management and their stakeholders. One perspective stresses the importance of stakeholder engagement, while the other stresses the importance of internal change management. Zollo *et al.* (2009) argue that even though the two components are part of the same definition, they each describe different types of activities. While activities related to internal change management are internal, activities related to stakeholders are external. While activities related to stakeholders are conducted at the periphery of the organization, internal change management is carried out at the core of the organization.

Zollo *et al.* (2009) studied the influence of the two perspectives on the quality of social performance in business enterprises. They found that internal change management had the strongest influence on social performance. Perceptions of corporate social performance were measured in terms of level of social performance as judged by interviewees.

The positive result related to the internal change management perspective is interpreted by Zollo *et al.* (2009) as additional evidence of the importance played by organizational capabilities dedicated to the management of internal change. Internal change is important in the business enterprise's ongoing quest to adapt to ever-changing environmental expectations and pressures. Firms that integrate corporate social responsibility into business processes may develop better cognitive alignment as a result, and firms with greater cognitive alignment may be more inclined to integrate responsibility into business processes.

Organizational change requires leadership. D'Amato and Roome (2009) developed a framework of leadership for corporate responsibility and sustainable development. Important elements in the framework are:

1. Developing vision, strategy and policies including practices such as grounding the company vision for global responsibility in its context.
2. Making corporate social responsibility operational by practices that make global responsibility part of everyday processes and procedures, and that integrate actions across business lines and locations.
3. Top management supporting adequate resourcing for global responsibility projects, creation of dedicated positions, and specific investment decisions.
4. Engaging across boundaries internally and externally. There is a need to work across personal boundaries of social identity,

internal boundaries of level and function, and structural boundaries of organization country or region.

5. Empowerment and development of stakeholders to become more globally responsible, such as enhancing individual power to properly promote and perform global responsibility.
6. Communication for corporate responsibility comprises the development of policies and procedures to effectively collect and share information.
7. Performance development and accountability to encourage global responsibility efforts and hold individuals and groups accountable for their contributions.
8. Acting ethically with integrity sets an example inside and outside the company that global responsibility is taken seriously.

D'Amato and Roome (2009) argue that by isolating effective leadership practices, it is possible then to identify required competencies and skills for the CEO and other corporate executives. This is in line with research by Mostovicz *et al.* (2009) that stress the important role of leadership in driving ethical outcomes. They argue that the different approaches to corporate social responsibility are not necessarily ethical since ethics is based on the knowledge and ethical involvement of the actor.

Since leadership can be conceptualized as the emotional ability to follow one's worldview, rather than a hierarchical position, knowledge combined with involved attitude and interest is an important requirement in management. Furthermore, executives need to replace their micro view with a macro view, and their short-term view with a long-term view. The macro view argues that CSR is interwoven into the organization's fabric and cannot be addressed separately from the organization's other goals. This view claims that organizations have a moral obligation toward society and their goals range from economic to social and environmental ones. The long-term view not only considers the organization as an entity whose purpose is far beyond the narrow for-profit perspective, but argues that the organization's responsibility should be past, present and future oriented. The ultimate goal of an organization is sustainability (Mostovicz *et al.*, 2009).

An example of a demanding internal change management situation is a merger. A company's social responsibility to employees during a merger is a challenging task for executive management. A company may ignore its non-obligatory responsibilities to employees during a major change such as a merger, leading to their disaffection and feeling of insecurity. In a study conducted by Chun (2009), perceptions of organizational empathy, warmth and conscientiousness were strongly correlated with employee loyalty, perceived job security, satisfaction and emotional attachment. Also, employees from the acquiring companies had a more negative feeling towards the merged organization, which is contrary to that expected from existing literature.

Aldama *et al.* (2009) suggest embedding corporate responsibility through effective organizational structure. They argue that integrating the corporate responsibility function has become a must for companies if they wish to remain competitive in the markets they act. They found that the way in which companies are integrating the corporate responsibility function varies, and that the old adage "structure follows strategy" does not always seem to be the rule.

Stages of Corporate Social Responsibility

Some business enterprises are more advanced than other enterprises in the area of corporate social responsibility. Such differences can be conceptualized in terms of stages of growth for organizational maturity, where the extent of learning is an important characteristic of higher stages of growth.

Maturity levels in terms of stages of growth models have been used widely in both organizational research and information technology management research. According to King and Teo

Figure 2.   Stage Model for Maturity in Corporate Social Responsibility.

(1997), these models describe a wide variety of phenomena — the organizational life cycle, product life cycle, biological growth, and so forth. These models assume that predictable patterns (conceptualized in terms of stages) exist in the growth of organizations, the sales levels of products, the diffusion of information technology, and the growth of living organisms. These stages are (i) sequential in nature, (ii) occur as a hierarchical progression that is not easily reversed, and (iii) involve a broad range of organizational activities and structures.

Castello and Lozano (2009) developed a stage model for corporate social responsibility as illustrated in Figure 2.

There are three stages in the model adapted from Castello and Lozano (2009):

➤ *Stage 1. Risk Management.* This is a base stage where corporate social responsibility is seen as a tool to protect reputation value. Within risk management, firms start to develop systems to measure and control environmental and social issues and threats. These control systems involve the planning and social forecasting, preparing for social response and development of the first set of corporate social policies.

➢ *Stage 2. Responsibility Management.* Business enterprises change their business processes and control mechanisms to reflect social and environmental responsibilities. Social issue management is proactive and systematic, often through the use of publicly accepted performance standards. There is often a need for a change in authority structure so corporate social responsibility departments are created.

➢ *Stage 3. Civil Management.* At this stage, the business enterprise is focusing on its citizenship as a civil corporation. The enterprise is open to integrating social issues as part of their responsibilities, assuming a citizenship role in leading social issues and transforming their business models to achieve this objective. This transformation is often driven by the internal redefinition of the company's role, mission and vision to the corporate social responsibility values. The span and depth of responsibility programs often drive social innovation, which benefits firms and the communities they operate in. Management systems are developed to monitor targets related to the improvement of environmental and social impacts.

Castello and Lozano (2009) identified several factors that drive the evolution from the risk stage via the responsibility stage to the civil stage. They acknowledge the importance of management systems as a major factor in the development of corporate social responsibility change. Codes of conduct, measurement systems, responsibility policies, and audits are the most common systems. Furthermore, policies and management systems need to be supported by active programs to help companies create an identity around them.

At stage 2, corporate social responsibility departments are often created. A study by Jacopin and Fontrodona (2009) questions the corporate social responsibility department's alignment with the business model of the company to provide some insights concerning the strategic focus of the department. The study shows that embedding responsibility into the organization is one of the most challenging issues in corporate responsibility today.

Stages of growth models have been criticized for a lack of empirical validity. Benbasat *et al.* (1984) found that most of the benchmark variables for stages used by Nolan (1979) were not confirmed in empirical studies. Based on empirical evidence, Benbasat *et al.* (1984) wrote the following critique of Nolan's stage hypothesis.

The stage hypothesis on the assimilation of computing technology provides one of the most popular models for describing and managing the growth of administrative information systems. Despite little formal evidence of its reliability or robustness, it has achieved a high level of acceptance among practitioners. We describe and summarize the findings of seven empirical studies conducted during the past six years that tested various hypotheses derived from this model. The accumulation of evidence from these studies casts considerable doubt on the validity of the stage hypothesis as an explanatory structure for the growth of computing in organizations.

For example, Nolan (1979) proposed that steering committees should be constituted in later stages of maturity. However, an empirical study showed that of 114 firms, 64 of which had steering committees, the correlation between IT maturity and steering committees was not significant (Benbasat *et al.*, 1984). In practice, organizations adopt steering committees throughout the development cycle rather than in the later stages.

Another example is charge-back methods. In a survey, approximately half of the firms used charge-back systems and the other half did not. In the Nolan (1979) structure, as firms mature through later stages, they should have adopted charge-back systems. Yet, in the empirical analysis, there were no significant correlations between maturity indicators and charge-back system usage, according to Benbasat *et al.* (1984). Benchmark variables such as steering committees and charge-back systems have to be carefully selected and tested before they are applied in survey research.

The concept of stages of growth has created a number of skeptics. Some argue that the concept of an organization progressing unidirectionally through a series of predictable stages is overly simplistic. For example, organizations may evolve through periods of convergence and divergence related more to shifts in information technology than to issues of growth for specific IT. According to Kazanjian and Drazin (1989), it can be argued that firms do not necessarily demonstrate any inexorable momentum to progress through a linear sequence of stages, but rather that observed configurations of problems, strategies, structures and processes will determine firms' progress.

Kazanjian and Drazin (1989) addressed the need for further data-based research to empirically examine whether organizations in a growth environment shift according to a hypothesized stage of growth model, or whether they follow a more random pattern of change associated with shifts in configurations that do not follow such a progression. Based on a sample of 71 firms they found support for the stage hypothesis.

For several decades, there has been a need to validate the stage model hypothesis both theoretically and empirically. Furthermore, there is a need for benchmark variables that will have different content for different stages. The alternative is to apply dominant problems and identify how they change from one stage to the next. Also, pros (strengths) and cons (weaknesses) to suggested models have to be taken into account. There is definitely a need to provide a more critical analysis of stage models and solve some of the basic issues that are long overdue.

This is a valuable effort. Rather than thinking of knowledge management technology or other efforts in terms of alternative strategies, the stage thinking suggests an evolutionary approach where the future is building on the past, rather than the future being a divergent path from the past. Rather than thinking that what was done in the past is wrong, past actions are the only available foundation for future actions. If past actions are not on the path to success, direction is changed without history being reversed.

Chapter 8
Forensic Accounting

Enron is one of the most famous accounting scandals in the world. Enron shareholders have recovered only a small fraction of their losses from the sudden demise of the company in 2001 and the company's resulting bankruptcy. Pearson (2010: 18) argues that the accounting profession needs to be a leader in white-collar prevention and detection:

> The accounting profession should consistently speak loudly opposing fraud and lack of accountability for third parties who participate in a fraudulent scheme. The profession should feel an ethical responsibility to help investors and lead the fight against securities fraud. The profession is engaging in short term thinking when it seeks legal immunity for all third parties involved in a fraudulent scheme. Thus, the accounting profession should voice opposition to fraud, even when it might result in slightly higher potential legal liability for the profession.

The author of this book conducted a survey on white-collar crime in 2010. Some of the respondents mentioned accounting:

> "Executives are in charge of control mechanisms and management accounting. When they themselves commit financial crime, they manipulate internal control and management auditing"
> "You need to get into the details, often single items in an invoice, to be able to detect misconduct. Very often it is difficult to find tracks in accounting systems"

Hansen (2009) argues that accounting and computer forensics are currently the investigators' best tools in detection and implemented in most white-collar investigations in recent years. Applications of science and technology to white-collar crime cases is increasing, and advances in technology have led to a greater dependence on expert testimony in white-collar crime cases, keeping in mind that expert opinion cannot be given with absolute certainty.

Investigative Accounting

Forensic accounting is the use of accounting information for law enforcement. It is the use of intelligence techniques in accounting to develop information for legal purposes. The term "forensic" refers to objects that are used as proofs. The term "investigative" refers to a goal-oriented approach of finding out what has happened. The term "accounting" refers to activities that include identifying, recording, settling, extracting, sorting, reporting, and verifying financial data (Crumbley *et al.*, 2007).

According to Crumbley *et al.* (2007: 1), there is a difference between the term forensic accounting and the term fraud auditing:

> A fraud auditor is an accountant specially skilled in auditing who is generally engaged in auditing with a view toward fraud discovery, documentation, and prevention. A forensic accountant may take on fraud auditing engagements and may in fact be a fraud auditor, but he or she will also use other accounting, consulting, and legal skills in broader engagements. In addition to the accounting and investigative skills that should certainly be present in the fraud auditor, the forensic accountant needs a working knowledge of the legal system and excellent quantitative analysis and communication skills to carry out expert testimony in the courtroom and to aid in other litigation support engagements.

Forensic accountants are essential to the legal system, providing expert services such as fake invoicing valuations, suspicious bankruptcy valuations, and analysis of financial documents in fraud schemes (Curtis, 2008).

Forensic accounting as a discipline has its own models and methodologies of investigative procedures that search for assurance, attestation and advisory perspectives to produce legal evidence. It is concerned with the evidentiary nature of accounting data, and as a practical field is concerned with accounting fraud and forensic auditing; compliance, due diligence, and risk assessment; detection of financial statement misrepresentation and financial statement fraud (Skousen and Wright, 2008); tax evasion; bankruptcy and valuation studies; violations of accounting regulations; non-standard entries, structured transactions, records tampering, and earnings mismanagement.

Forensic accountants apply decision aids as well as professional judgment in their work (Chan *et al.*, 2008). Decision aids are technology and systems that offer the potential to improve detection of white-collar crime in accounting. Hughes *et al.* (2008) argue that strong corporate control environments are critical to responsible and reliable detection of misconduct.

Financial crime such as fraud can be subject to forensic accounting, since fraud encompasses the acquisition of property or economic advantage by means of deception, through either a misrepresentation or concealment. Forensic examinations include consideration of digital evidence, including communications (Curtis, 2008).

To develop investigative knowledge in the area of forensic accounting, Kranacher *et al.* (2008) suggest a model curriculum consisting of several concepts such as basic accounting, basic auditing, transaction processing, business law, business communication and computer skills. The purpose of such a curriculum is to build knowledge, skills and abilities in forensic accounting to combat white-collar crime.

Accounting in general, and forensic accounting in particular (Baird and Zelin, 2009), are important investigative tools for detection of white-collar crime. However, Carnegie and Napier (2010: 360) found that society's perception of the legitimacy of the accounting profession and accounting professionals has suffered after scandals such as Enron:

> The unexpected collapse of Enron and the bewildering demise of Arthur Andersen in the aftermath sent shock waves through the

accounting profession worldwide. The impact of Enron's collapse was greater because it was closely followed by the bankruptcy of WorldCom in the USA, while scandals and collapses involving companies such as HIH Insurance in Australia, Parmalat in Italy, Royal Ahold in the Netherlands and Equitable Life Assurance Society in the UK showed that this was not just a US phenomenon. "Enronitis" became a label associated with highly questionable accounting and auditing practices. Although these practices were widely condemned as they became public knowledge, they sharply undermined confidence in corporate financial reporting and auditing as well as corporate regulation.

As a consequence, accountants have to deal with a growing mix of new rules on corporate governance, audit independence and financial reporting. Carnegie and Napier (2010) applied legitimacy and social contract theory to portray such consequences for the accounting profession after Enron. According to the legitimacy theory, business organizations are part of a broader social system and do not possess an inherent right to own or use resources or even to exist. Society confers legitimacy upon an organization, where legitimacy is defined as a condition or status, which exists when an entity's value system is congruent with the value system of the larger social system of which the entity is a part. Under social contract theory, the basic morality is adherence to uniform social accords that serve the best interests of those entering into agreement. Social contract theory is concerned with showing how individual and social group rights and liberties are founded on mutually advantageous agreements between members of society.

Forensic accounting is dependent on a link between accounting information and intelligence management. Despite calls to link management accounting generally more closely to management, Hall (2010) found that much is still to be learned about the role of accounting information in managerial work. Similarly, much is still to be learned about the role of forensic accounting in white-collar detection, prevention and strategy in business enterprises.

Cases of Forensic Audit

Huefner (2010: 2) tells the story of a forensic audit in the public sector:

> In September 2002, the Roslyn Union Free School District's external auditor — a small local (Long Island) CPA firm known as Miller, Lilly and Pearce — received information from an undisclosed source that the District was purchasing numerous items from a local Home Depot store, items that did not seem to be of the type that a school district might normally buy. The CPA firm contacted the audit committee chair of the Board of Education, and an inquiry was authorized. Attention immediately focused on Pamela Gluckin, the assistant superintendent for business — the chief financial officer in a school district. Evidence regarding $30,166 in suspect purchases from Home Depot was found in her files.
>
> CPA firm personnel apparently then spent one day, October 16, 2002, examining district records. While little documentation apparently was retained regarding this review, the CPA later described the process to the state auditors. The audit process involved downloading all transactions that had been personally entered by Ms. Gluckin (rather than by the usual accounting personnel) and examining the supporting documentation. In addition to the $30,166 of Home Depot charges, this review yielded a list of undocumented payments to 12 additional vendors aggregating $192,970, for a total of $223,136 to 13 vendors.
>
> Upon the recommendation of both the CPA firm and an attorney recommended by District superintendent Frank Tassone, the Board agreed to accept restitution of $250,000 — the $223,136 loss plus $26,864 in accounting and legal fees — along with the retirement of Ms. Gluckin and her surrender of her administrator's license. No criminal charges would be pursued, and no public announcement would be made. The matter appeared to be closed.

But the matter was not closed (Huefner, 2010: 3):

> A little over a year later, in early 2004, further allegations arose that the Roslyn fraud was more extensive and more widespread — both in terms of the time frame and in terms of people involved — than had been determined earlier. The local (Nassau County) district attorney began an investigation and then the State Comptroller's

Office began an audit on June 1, 2004. This audit soon determined that the theft exceeded $11 million. Pamela Gluckin, who had resigned in 2002, was arrested on charges that she stole in excess of $1 million. Soon after, both Superintendent Frank Tassone and account clerk Deborah Rigano (who happened to be Pamela Gluckin's niece) both resigned. They were later arrested on charges of first and second degree grand larceny.

Neumann *et al.* (2010: 1) tell the story of a forensic audit of staffing and census in a long-term care facility:

Butler Long-Term Care was a 60-bed nursing home certified to provide care to residents requiring a substantially greater quantity and quality of skilled nursing care compared to residents at ordinary nursing homes. BLTC is a fictitious name assigned to maintain confidentiality. The Federal government audited BLTC and concluded that inflated invoices had been submitted for patient services because BLTC was inadequately staffed as required in statutory and regulatory requirements.

The forensic audit started by searching staffing data in sign-in sheets, staffing schedules, nursing departmental reports, and payroll record. Payroll records were found to be the most reliable data set available. They found direct nursing hours invoiced to be substantially higher than direct nursing hours registered. The case was settled for less than two million dollars, which was an amount approximately equal to the government's costs in the case (Neumann *et al.*, 2010).

Deception Detection

Accountants often have longstanding associations with white-collar personnel in a corporation and may therefore have expanded capabilities to detect potential white-collar crime among executives. A study by Lee and Welker (2010) suggests that personal familiarity enhances deception-detection ability. However, their findings additionally suggest that the enhanced deception-detection ability may be confined to the context in which the familiarity was acquired.

Lee and Welker (2010) suggest that accountants may be qualified for investigative interviewing because of their associations with suspects. Familiarity with an interviewee's communicative style, acquired from multiple exposures to an interviewee when telling the truth as well as presenting white lies, might enhance the detector's ability to detect the interviewee's white lies. Accountant interviewers can acquire familiarity with the interviewee's communicative style by observing truth telling and white lying in a situation where the interviewer passively listens to, but not necessarily interacts with, the interviewee.

It is an interesting accountant role of passive interviewer suggested by Lee and Welker (2010) in the detection and prevention of white-collar crime, because interviews are generally the main source of information in most investigations. In police investigations, interviews are performed by means of interrogation of witnesses, suspects, reference persons and experts, and information is collected on crime, criminals, time and place, organizations, relationships, criminal projects, all kinds of activities, and criminal entrepreneurship. Therefore, combinations of information sources such as document studies and number checking can be further expanded to interviews and observations, so that behavioral aspects are integrated into forensic accounting (Ramamoorti, 2008).

Lee and Welker (2010) based their suggestions on their experimental study that assessed whether familiarity with an interviewee's communicative style improves an interviewers' ability to detect deception. In the experimental treatment, interviewers observed interviewees as they told truths and white lies over the course of ten weeks. During this period, the accuracy of detecting white lies increased from sixty-one percent to eighty-one percent.

Deception detection is important. Deception represents lying, and deception detection is the ability to make judgments of truths versus lies. Ariail *et al.* (2010) argue that knowledge of deception detection techniques can improve both accountants' and auditors' abilities to evaluate verbal responses to audit inquiries. Such knowledge gives accountants and auditors an additional tool by which to lessen detection risk.

Ariail *et al.* (2010) identified four general deception detection guidelines that can assist in the evaluation of verbal responses to audit inquiries. First, investigators need the recognizing that no single behavior — such as avoiding eye contact — indicates deception all the time. Next, listening to what person says rather than how or he looks when saying. Third, not leading an interviewee, but rather let the person talk. Finally, investigators need to compare a suspect's statement to other reliable information.

Analytical Procedures

Analytical procedures to detect white-collar crime by means of forensic accounting involve the comparison of relationships between two or more measures for the purpose of establishing the reasonableness of each one compared. Crumbley *et al.* (2003) suggest five types of analytical procedures that help find unusual magnitudes or relationships, errors, or fraud: horizontal, vertical, variance, ratio and comparative analysis. These kinds of analytical procedures reveal where to go to audit and what the investigator might search for. Percentage analysis is applied in both horizontal and vertical procedures that help detect financial statement fraud identifiers and red flags.

Crumbley *et al.* (2003) describe the five types of analytical procedures as follows:

➢ *Horizontal analysis* assists in the search of inequalities by using the financial statements of some prior year as the base and expressing the components of a future year as percentages of each component in the base year. This technique may be used for balance sheet and income statement comparison, and to some extent in the analysis of the statement of cash flow. Typically, horizontal analysis starts with a base year, and each successive year is compared with the base year. The significant changes in account balances from period to period are investigated to determine the reason for the change.

➤ *Vertical analysis* presents every item in a statement as a percentage of the largest item in the statement. For example, in using the income statement, net sales are usually expressed as 100% and all other items are compared with net sales. The largest item on the balance sheet is total assets, which is expressed as 100%, and the statement of cash flows usually applies the change in cash as the base.

➤ *Variance analysis* is concerned with the difference between a budgeted, planned or expected amount and the actual amount incurred. The variance for one item may be surprisingly large, and the variance for some items may be significantly larger than the variance for other items.

➤ *Ratio analysis* is a subset of trend analysis that can be used to compare relationships among financial statement accounts at one specific point in time as well as over time to find the fakes. A ratio expresses the magnitude of quantities relative to each other.

➤ *Comparative analysis* presents comparisons of measures from different sources. Comparative analysis is about comparing and contrasting two or more figures. In the "lens" (or "keyhole") comparison, in which a measure A is assigned less weight than measure B, A can be used as a lens through which to view B. Lens comparisons are useful for illuminating, critiquing, or challenging the stability of an item that, before analysis, seemed perfectly reasonable.

Suspicious Transactions

The proceeds of crime find their ways into different sectors of the economy. Money laundering means the securing of the proceeds of a criminal act. Suspicious transactions reporting are one of the most important obligations of financial systems to disclose and prevent the laundering of money from criminal acts. If financial institutions suspect that funds are connected to criminal activity, they should be permitted or required to promptly report their suspicions to the competent authorities. The obligation to report suspicious transactions has been widely accepted in many countries (Ping, 2005).

Many countries are introducing legislation to combat money laundering. Norway got its Money Laundering Act in 2009. The purpose of the act is to prevent and detect transactions associated with proceeds of crime or associated with acts of terrorism. According to the act, many entities have an obligation to report suspicious transactions, such as banks, law firms, real estate agents, and dealers in movable property such as auctioneers. If an entity with a reporting obligation suspects that a transaction is associated with proceeds of crime, then further enquiries have to be made by the entity to confirm or disprove the suspicion.

Money Laundering

Money laundering is a sort of criminal activity that tries to conceal the illegality of proceeds of crime by disguising them as lawful earnings (He, 2010). Money laundering is an example of financial crime often carried out as white-collar crime (Abramova, 2007; Council of Europe, 2007; Elvins, 2003). Money laundering means the securing of the proceeds of a criminal act (Ping, 2005). The proceeds must be integrated into the legal economy before the perpetrators can use it. The purpose of laundering is to make it appear as if the proceeds were acquired legally, as well as disguise its illegal origins (EFE, 2008). Money laundering takes place within all types of profit-motivated crime, such as embezzlement, fraud, misappropriation, corruption, robbery, distribution of narcotic drugs and trafficking in human beings (Økokrim, 2008).

Money laundering has often been characterized as a three-stage process that requires (i) moving the funds from direct association with the crime, (ii) disguising the trail to foil pursuit, and (iii) making them available to the criminal once again with their occupational and geographic origins hidden from view. The first stage is the most risky one for the criminals, since money from crime is introduced into the financial system. Stage 1 is often called the placement stage. Stage 2 is often called the layering stage, in which money is moved in order to disguise or remove direct links to the offence committed. The money may be channeled through several transactions, which could involve a number of accounts, financial institutions, companies and funds as well as the use of professionals such as lawyers, brokers and consultants as intermediaries. Stage 3 is often called the integration stage, where a legitimate basis for asset origin has been created. The money is made available to the criminal and can be used freely for private consumption, luxury purchases, real estate investment or investment in legal businesses.

Money laundering has also been described as a five-stage process: placement, layering, integration, justification, and embedding (Stedje, 2004). Money laundering is a complicated activity, in which the source and nature of dirty money are disguised in order to make the money look lawful and then become useable, transferable, and negotiable (He, 2010).

It has also been suggested that money laundering falls outside of the category of financial crime. Since money-laundering activities may use the same financial system that is used for the perpetration of core financial crime, its overlap with the latter is apparent (Stedje, 2004).

According to Joyce (2005), criminal money is frequently removed from the country in which the crime occurred to be cycled through the international payment system to obscure any audit trail. The third stage of money laundering is done in different ways. For example, a credit card might be issued by offshore banks, casino "winnings" can be cashed out, capital gains on option and stock trading might occur, and real estate sale might cause profit.

The proceeds of criminal acts could be generated from organized crime such as drug trafficking, people smuggling, people trafficking, proceeds from robberies or money acquired by embezzlement, tax evasion, fraud, abuse of company structures, insider trading or corruption. The EFE (2008) in Norway argues that most criminal acts are motivated by profit. When crime generates significant proceeds, the perpetrators need to find a way to control the assets without attracting attention to themselves or the offence committed. Thus, the money laundering process is decisive in order to enjoy the proceeds without arousing suspicion.

The proceeds of crime find their ways into different sectors of the economy. A survey in Canada indicates that deposit institutions are the single largest recipient, having being identified in 114 of the 149 proceeds of crime (POC) cases (Schneider, 2004). While the insurance sector was implicated in almost 65% of all cases, in the vast majority the offender did not explicitly seek out the insurance sector as a laundering device. Instead, because motor vehicles, homes, companies, and marine vessels were purchased with the proceeds of crime, it was often necessary to purchase insurance for these assets.

He (2010) developed a typology of money laundering techniques, and these are three examples:

➢ *Cash smuggling* is a method of money laundering in which the proceeds of crime are illegally moved cross border, and then deposited in banking institutions, used to pay for real estate or invested in local companies.

➢ *Bank depositing* is a method of money laundering where crime money can be transformed into other currencies, loans, discounts, and settlements. Criminals transfer capital through transferring accounts or remiting funds into other sectors.

➢ *Insurance claiming* is a method where the criminal is first buying, then altering and surrendering insurance policies and then filing insurance claim.

➢ *Real estate and lottery buying* is a method of acquiring valuables that can later be sold. For example, prize-winning lotteries can be bought by criminals from the winner, and then be cashed in by the criminal from the lottery administration.

He (2010) describes many more laundering techniques. He argues that money laundering exists almost everywhere. Taking advantage of different financial and legal systems of different countries, money laundering has transnational dimensions. Under the cover of legal financial activities, money laundering is a very secret crime.

Transaction Criteria

It is not obvious what is meant by suspicious transactions. Therefore, the criteria of suspicious transactions vary from country to country. Current reporting systems can be roughly divided into two main types (Ping, 2005):

➢ *Transaction Size.* Financial transactions above a threshold amount are reported by the system to law enforcement agencies, whether or not the transaction is felt to be suspect. Such a system leaves less to the discretion of entities or persons, thereby promoting uniformity and consistency in enforcement. This is called the objective model.
➢ *Suspicion Size.* Financial transactions that are considered as suspicious are reported by the system to law enforcement agencies. This is called the subjective model. The judgment should be based on a combination of factors, such as the personality of the customer, his behavior, the type and terms of the transaction asked for, and whether the transaction is a usual one or not.

A combination of the objective model and the subjective model is called the hybrid model. The system can preserve the best attributes of the objective and subjective models. The objective model has its strength in uniformity and consistency in enforcement, and its weakness in much useless information. It may be exploited by criminals to sidestep the laws and is also incapable of persuading relevant entities and persons to play an active role in the fight against money laundering. The subjective model has its strength in personal judgment of behavior and transaction, and its weakness in staff lacking sufficient expertise. The hybrid model can be implemented as a system of unusual transactions reporting rather than suspicious transactions reporting (Ping, 2005).

Suspicious transactions reporting are growing in most countries, where a financial intelligence unit is at the receiving end of such reports. The volume of data is growing, and financial intelligence units are applying computer systems to manipulate data for analysis purposes. With computerization, a considerable change has occurred.

Demetis (2009) found that computerization has led to a drop in hit-rate. While face-to-face interactions with clients are 60–70% more likely to bring about a suspicious transaction report that is deemed truly suspicious after manual analysis, only 5–10% are deemed truly suspicious after selection by anti money laundering software.

Many countries are members of the Financial Action Task Force that has established a number of recommendations (FATF, 2004). According to these recommendations, a financial institution is required to report promptly when it has reasonable grounds to suspect that funds are proceeds of a criminal activity. Countries should establish financial intelligence units that serve as national centers for the receiving, analysis and dissemination of suspicious transaction reports.

Member states within FATF exchange information and experience of laundering types. For example, the red-flag approach to money laundering in the insurance sector may include identification of activities such as: (i) the purchase of an insurance product inconsistent with the customer's needs; (ii) unusual payment methods, such as cash, cash equivalents (when such a usage of cash or cash equivalents is, in fact, unusual), or structured monetary instruments; (iii) early termination of a product (including during the "free look" period), especially at a cost to the customer, or where payment is made by, or the refund check is directed to, an apparently unrelated third party; (iv) the transfer of the benefit of a product to an apparently unrelated third party; (v) a customer who shows little concern for the investment performance of a product, but a great deal of concern about the early termination features of the product; (vi) a customer who is reluctant to provide identifying information when purchasing a product, or who provides minimal or seemingly fictitious information; and (vii) a customer who borrows the maximum amount available soon after purchasing the product.

Information Processing

Suspicion of crime is based on information. Information is collected and analyzed to confirm or reject suspicion. Analysis of information from a criminal perspective is often called profiling. Selective information is both isolated and associated in profiling work for the purpose of detecting money laundering. Relationships are sought between information that can develop into a profile of the potential crime and the potential criminal.

Demetis (2009) argues that the growing volume of data that needs to be analyzed creates a problem for information manipulation. While humans are best at applying subjective and complex thinking when searching information, computers can perform standard searches much faster. Both humans and computer systems are looking to find the few suspicious transactions from a pool of millions.

Demetis (2009: 356) applies information theory to discuss information search and association where complexity is dependent on how meaning is constructed from information:

> A key problem that arises here has to do with the construction of the profiling queries themselves (i.e., the means we use to reduce complexity). It is doubtful whether the relationships that are uncovered by profiling are meaningful insofar as they target a problem domain (be that marketing, identity checks or financial

transactions for money laundering). The question further rises whether the relationships that are uncovered within the profiled-data are a byproduct of the profiling queries that prescribe the relationships to begin with.

Often, computer and human profiling become structurally coupled and co-dependent. However, Demetis (2009: 356) argues that what happens in the interaction between human and computer is not only heavily asymmetric in human disfavor, but also constructs a delusion:

> We are in fact used to believing that the keywords we type in will provide us with an accurate representation of web-reality even though we merrily disregard the hundreds of thousands or millions of results that lay in the background. Roughly, 90% of us do not get past the top ten. This does not only indicate an unquestioned belief in the functionality of algorithms through which our reality becomes constructed; but it also simply demonstrates that this is the mode of human processing; the mode of how we filter the world of computational complexity.

The same applies to any money laundering detection software where the vastness of transaction data has to be reduced. Software is a constructed reduction of complexity, and advanced human judgment becomes irrelevant since it is not part of the system until after the fact of complexity reduction.

An example can be found in Norway, where the financial intelligence unit uses a computer system called "Ask" (EFE, 2009). Ask is a system that handles receipt of suspicious transactions reports from banks and other organization. Ask conducts computer analysis of reports and presents conclusions. An algorithm is weighing information based on rules and searching for more information by means of navigators.

It is important to understand the limitations and dangers of a system such as Ask. Complexity reduction and simple calculations create a danger of most suspicious transactions being ignored by the system. In systems, theoretical terms such as "distinction" and "difference" are left to algorithms to decide. Information gets lost in noise. Also humans have limited capacity to process information and need to manipulate it, but curiosity and creativity are human attributes that increase the likelihood of discovering money laundering transactions (Neuser, 2005; Tong, 2007).

Every act of observation, such as reading a suspicious transaction report, is based on making distinctions. To observe is to create a distinction between what can be observed and, automatically, what must by necessity be left unobserved. At the core of a system to detect money laundering, the fundamental code that creates this distinction is based on the communicable form of a report, thus designating what is suspicious and non-suspicious (Demetis, 2009).

Demetis (2009) suggests the concept of electreaucracy to encapsulate the problem of systemic interferences by technology. In electreaucracy, technology becomes the modern underlying fabric where distinctions become subsumed from every problem domain that is affected by technology and/or utilizes technology for a purpose. Electreaucracy is about the organization of informational elements on the basis of the fundamental code of automation/ non-automation. Profiling software that attempt to simulate money-laundering behavior cannot account for the forceful reduction in complexity carried out by human profiling.

Chapter 9
Knowledge Management

Prevention of white-collar crime and protection of corporate reputation require knowledge management. Knowledge management is a systematic and integrative process of coordinating organization-wide knowledge sharing and knowledge development to reach organizational goals such as improved corporate reputation. Knowledge management encompasses the managerial efforts in facilitating activities of acquiring, creating, storing, sharing, diffusing, developing, and deploying knowledge by individuals and groups. Knowledge management practices need to fit with organizational context in order to make a difference. Practices of knowledge management are context-specific, and they can influence organizational effectiveness (Zheng *et al.*, 2010).

Zheng *et al.* (2010) studied the possible mediating role of knowledge management in the relationship between organizational culture, structure, strategy, and organizational effectiveness. Their results suggest that knowledge management fully mediates the impact of organizational culture on organizational effectiveness, and partially mediates the impact of organizational structure and strategy on organizational effectiveness.

Knowledge Organization

Knowledge is considered an important resource in most firms. The resource-based view of the firm posits that firm competitiveness comes from unique bundles of tangible and intangible assets that are valuable, rare, imperfectly imitable, non-substitutable, combinable and sustainable (Zheng *et al.*, 2010).

Knowledge organization has emerged as the dominant structure of both public and private organizations in the transition from an industrial to a knowledge society (Lassen *et al.*, 2006). Knowledge organization in the management sciences is concerned with structures within which knowledge workers solve knowledge problems (Bennet, 2005a, 2005b; Bergström *et al.*, 2009; Lassen *et al.*, 2006; Smith, 2003; Uretsky, 2001).

There are many definitions of knowledge. Nonaka *et al.* (2000) describe it as justified true belief. Definitions of organizational knowledge range from a complex, accumulated expertise that resides in individuals and is partly or largely inexpressible, to a much more structured and explicit content. There are also several classifications of knowledge, e.g., far, explicit, embodied, encoded, embedded, event, procedural, and common. Knowledge has long been recognized as a valuable resource for organizational growth and sustained competitive advantage, especially for organizations competing in uncertain environments. Recently, some researchers have argued that knowledge is an organization's most valuable resource because it represents intangible assets, operational routines, and creative processes that are hard to imitate (Wasko and Faraj, 2005). However, the effective management of knowledge is fundamental to the organization's ability to create and sustain competitive advantage.

Knowledge management research has described organizational knowledge flows in terms of the knowledge circulation process, consisting of five components: knowledge creation, accumulation, sharing, utilization and internalization. Of these five parts, the knowledge sharing process is what this book focuses on. Knowledge sharing within and between organizations is not a one-way activity, but a process of trial and error, feedback, and mutual adjustment of both the source and the recipient of knowledge. This mutuality in the knowledge sharing suggests that the process can be constructed as a sequence of collective actions in which the source and the recipient are involved. There are many different knowledge sharing mechanisms: it can be informal and personal as well as formal and impersonal. Informal mechanisms include talk, unscheduled meetings, electronic bulletin boards, and discussion databases. More formal knowledge sharing channels include video conferencing, training sessions, organizational intranets, and databases.

Bennet and Bennet (2005a) define knowledge organizations as complex adaptive systems composed of a large number of self-organizing components that seek to maximize their own goals but operate according to rules in the context of relationships with other components. In an intelligent complex adaptive system, the agents are people. The systems (organizations) are frequently composed of hierarchical levels of self-organizing agents (or knowledge workers), which can take the forms of teams, divisions or other structures that have common bonds. Thus while the components (knowledge workers) are self-organizing, they are not independent from the system they comprise (the professional organization).

Knowledge is often referred to as information combined with interpretation, reflection, and context. In cybernetics, knowledge is defined as a reducer of complexity or as a relation to predict and to select those actions that are necessary in establishing a competitive advantage for organizational survival. That is, knowledge is the capability to draw distinctions, within a domain of actions (Laise et al., 2005). According to the knowledge-based view of the organization, the uniqueness of an organization's knowledge plays a fundamental role in its sustained ability to perform and succeed (Turner and Makhija, 2006).

According to the knowledge-based theory of the firm, knowledge is the main resource for a firm's competitive advantage. Knowledge is the primary driver of a firm's value. Performance differences across firms can be attributed to the variance in the firms' strategic knowledge. Strategic knowledge is characterized by being valuable, unique, rare, non-imitable, non-substitutable, non-transferable, combinable, and exploitable. Unlike other inert organizational resources, the application of existing knowledge has the potential to generate new knowledge (Garud and Kumaraswamy, 2005).

Inherently, however, knowledge resides within individuals, more specifically, in the employees who create, recognize, archive, access, and apply knowledge in carrying out their tasks (Liu and Chen, 2005). Consequently, the movement of knowledge across individual and organizational boundaries is dependent on employees' knowledge sharing behaviors (Liebowitz, 2004). Bock *et al.* (2005) found that extensive knowledge sharing within organizations still appears to be the exception rather than the rule.

The knowledge organization is very different from the bureaucratic organization. For example, the knowledge organization's focus on flexibility and customer response is very different from the bureaucracy's focus on organizational stability and the accuracy and repetitiveness of internal processes. In the knowledge organization, current practices emphasize using the ideas and capabilities of employees to improve decision making and organizational effectiveness. In contrast, bureaucracies utilize autocratic decision making by senior leadership with unquestioned execution by the workforce (Bennet and Bennet, 2005b).

In knowledge organizations, transformational and charismatic leadership is an influential mode of leadership that is associated with high levels of individual and organizational performance. Leadership effectiveness is critically contingent on, and often defined in terms of, leaders' ability to motivate followers toward collective goals or a collective mission or vision. (Kark and Dijk, 2007).

In the knowledge society, knowledge organizations are expected to play a vital role in local economic development. For example, knowledge institutions such as universities are expected to stimulate regional and local economic development. Knowledge transfer units in universities such as Oxford in the UK and

Grenoble in France are responsible for local and regional innovations (Smith, 2003).

Uretsky (2001) argues that the real knowledge organization is the learning organization. A learning organization is one that changes as a result of its experiences. Under the best of circumstances, these changes result in performance improvements. The phrases "knowledge organization" and "learning organization" are usually (but not necessarily) used to describe service organizations. This is because most, if not all, of the value of these organizations comes from how well their professionals learn from the environment, diagnose problems, and then work with clients or customers to improve their situations. The problems with which they work are frequently ambiguous and unstructured. The information, skills, and experience needed to address these problems vary with work cases. A typical example is detectives in police investigations of white-collar crime.

Similarly, Bennet and Bennet (2005b) argue that learning and knowledge will have become two of the three most important emergent characteristics of the future world-class organization. Learning will be continuous and widespread, utilizing mentoring, classroom and distance learning, and will likely be self-managed with strong infrastructure support. The creation, storage, transfer, and application of knowledge will have been refined and developed such that it becomes a major resource of the organization as it satisfies customers and adapts to environmental and competitive forces and opportunities.

The third characteristic of future knowledge organizations will be that of organizational intelligence. Organizational intelligence is the ability of an organization to perceive, interpret and respond to its environment in a manner that meets its goals while satisfying multiple stakeholders. Intelligent behavior may be defined as being well prepared, providing excellent outcome-oriented thinking, choosing appropriate postures, and making outstanding decisions. Intelligent behavior includes acquiring knowledge continuously from all available resources and building it into an integrated picture, bringing together seemingly unrelated information to create new and unusual perspectives and to understand the surrounding world (Bennet and Bennet, 2005b).

In the context of policing and law enforcement, "intelligence" has another meaning as well. Brown (2007: 340) defines intelligence in this context as follows:

Intelligence is information, which is significant or potentially significant for an enquiry or potential enquiry.

What establishes information as intelligence is that it is a subset of information defined by the special quality of being significant and relevant. If information is significant, it has value and it has relevance. Analysis does not create intelligence; it merely discovers, attributes and refines it.

According to Bennet and Bennet (2005a), designing the knowledge organization of the future implies development of an intelligent complex adaptive system. In response to an environment of rapid change, increasing complexity and great uncertainty, the organization of the future must become an adaptive organic business. The intelligent complex adaptive system will enter into a symbiotic relationship with its cooperative enterprise, virtual alliances and external environment, while simultaneously retaining unity of purpose effective identification, and selection of incoming threats and opportunities.

In the knowledge organization, innovation and creativity are of critical importance. The literature on creativity provides a view of organizing for innovation by focusing on how individuals and teams come to shape knowledge in unique ways. Innovation consists of the creative generation of a new idea and the implementation of the idea into a valuable product, and thus creativity feeds innovation and is particularly critical in complex and interdependent work. Taylor and Greve (2006) argue that creativity can be viewed as the first stage of the overall innovation process.

Innovative solutions in the knowledge organization arise from diverse knowledge, processes that allow for creativity, and tasks directed toward creative solutions. Creativity requires application of deep knowledge because knowledge workers must understand the knowledge domain to push its boundaries. Team creativity likewise relies on tapping into the diverse knowledge of a team's members (Taylor and Greve, 2006).

Within knowledge organizations, we often find communities of practice. Brown and Duguid (2001) argue that for a variety of reasons, communities of practice seem to be a useful organizational subset for examining organizational knowledge as well as identity. First, such communities are privileged sites for a tight, effective loop of insight, problem identification, learning, and knowledge production. Second, they are significant repositories for the development, maintenance, and reproduction of knowledge. Third, community knowledge is more than the sum of its parts. Fourth, organizational ability to adapt to environmental change is often determined by communities of practice.

Business Intelligence

While data are numbers and letters without meaning, information is data in a context that makes sense. Information combined with interpretation, reflection and context is knowledge, while knowledge accumulated over time as learning is wisdom. In this hierarchical structure we find intelligence as more than information, while less than knowledge. Intelligence is analyzed information. In police work, intelligence can provide the basis for opening a new criminal case, it can be applied to the investigation of existing criminal cases, it can be used to reallocate investigative resources based on new crime patterns and actors, and it can be used for preventive measures.

In the private sector, a term called "business intelligence" has received substantial attention in recent years. Although different from police intelligence, business intelligence has some interesting perspectives for police intelligence as well (Laudon and Laudon, 2010; Williams and Williams, 2003).

Business intelligence is a process of taking large amounts of data, analyzing that data, and presenting a high-level set of reports that condense the essence of that data into the basis of business actions, enabling management to gain new insights and thereby contributing to their business decisions. Business intelligence is an interactive process that starts by assembling the data into a format conducive to analysis. Once the data are organized in a database, they must be checked and cleaned to correct errors and flaws. Once the information is retrieved to establish patterns or make predictions, models and hypotheses are tested and validated.

A series of tools enables users to analyze data to see new patterns, relationships, and structures that are useful for guiding investigations and decision making. Such tools for consolidating, analyzing, and providing access to vast amounts of data to help users improve business performance are referred to as business intelligence.

Business intelligence (BI) is an application of information technology (IT) that is used to extract critical business information for a growing number of functions. IT is used to process and analyze large amounts of data. IT is used for collection, treatment and diffusion of information that serves a purpose. Principle tools for business intelligence include software for database query and reporting, tools for multidimensional data analysis, and data mining.

Data have to be captured and organized before they are available for analysis. Data redundancy in terms of the presence of duplicate data should be avoided. Data inconsistency, where the same attribute may have different values, should be avoided as well. Rather than having traditional files where data are stored, it is much better to have data in databases, data warehouses, and data marts. Database technology cuts through many of the problems of traditional file organization. A database is a collection of data organized to serve many applications efficiently by centralizing the data and controlling redundant data (Laudon and Laudon, 2010: 240):

> Rather than storing data in separate files for each application, data are stored so as to appear to users as being stored in only one location. A single database services multiple applications.

A data warehouse is a database that stores current and historical data of potential interest to decision makers throughout the organization. The data originate in many core operational transaction systems, such as systems for sales, customer accounts, and manufacturing, and may include data from web site transactions. The data warehouse consolidates and standardizes information from different operational databases so that the information can be used across the enterprise for management analysis and decision making (Laudon and Laudon, 2010).

A data mart is a subset of a data warehouse in which a summarized or highly focused portion of the organization's data is placed in a separate database for a specific population of users. A data mart typically focuses on a single subject area or line of business, so it usually can be constructed more rapidly and at lower cost than an enterprise-wide data warehouse (Laudon and Laudon, 2010).

The following components constitute IT for BI:

➢ OLAP — On Line Analytical Processing. It refers to IT tools that allow for navigation in databases for hierarchies, relationships, developments and other perspectives. OLAP provides multidimensional and summarized views of business data and is used for modeling, analysis, reporting and planning of business activities. OLAP enables users to obtain online answers to ad hoc questions.
➢ Data Mining. This component takes advantage of statistical analysis techniques such as correlation analysis and regression analysis. Data mining is more discovery-driven than OLAP.
➢ Performance Management. For example, a balanced score card collects and exhibits performance in key areas such as finance, personnel, production, and market.

Similar to police intelligence, business intelligence is concerned with the identification of critical information for business performance. Business intelligence applications and their underlying critical information concepts support the needs of the business, provided they are tightly integrated to both business environment and information technology infrastructure (Williams and Williams, 2003).

In the hierarchical structure of data-information-knowledge-wisdom, we find intelligence as more than information and as less than knowledge. Intelligence is analyzed information, as illustrated in Figure 1. Here we use police investigation as an example.

Information and, to a similar extent, intelligence then consists of facts and other data which is organized to characterize or profile a particular situation, incident, or crime and the individual or group of individuals presumed to be involved. This organizing of the data to meaningful information of necessity involves some level of interpretation of the facts as presented. However, the role of interpretation here in information is relatively minor in comparison to its role in terms of knowledge construction. In this regard, the role

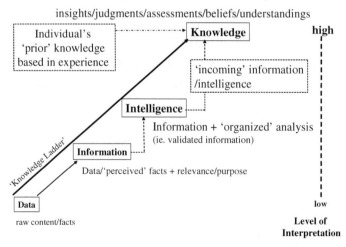

Figure 1. Hierarchy of Police Investigation Insight Expressed as a Continuum.

of interpretation in intelligence is greater and more explicit than in information, but not as full blown as in the making of knowledge.

Knowledge helps develop relevant meaning to information in intelligence work (Innes and Sheptycki, 2004: 6):

> The distinction between information and intelligence is well established, but can be difficult to grasp. Information consists of bits of data that, when combined and viewed together with relevant background knowledge, may be used to produce intelligence, which informs the actions and decisions of policing organizations.

Knowledge as implied operates at a higher level of abstraction and consists of judgments and assessments based in personal beliefs, truths, and expectations about the information received and how it is should be analyzed, evaluated and synthesized, in short — interpreted — so that it can be used and implemented into some form of action.

Stages of Growth

A knowledge organization is defined as an organization where the end product of work processes in the organization is knowledge or a service. If the end product of an organization is not a knowledge-based service while most or all work processes require advanced knowledge, such an organization is defined as a knowledge-intensive organization. While a knowledge-intensive organization might deliver goods such as food and transportation, a knowledge organization delivers a service, which is an intangible product.

A typical example of a knowledge organization is a law firm. A law firm is an organization specialized in the application of legal knowledge to client problems. The client may want to prevent a problem or solve a problem. In law firm work of prevention and solution, lawyers in the firm apply a variety of knowledge categories such as declarative knowledge and procedural knowledge. Many law firms have transformed themselves from a professional model to a corporate business model. Knowledge is perceived as the resource on which the business is based. Unique, non-imitable, combinable and exploitable knowledge provides competitive advantage. Thus, their primary resources stem from the human capital and social capital of the individuals employed within them.

"Business model" is an expression that has gained ground considerably in the last decade. This concept is applied both in private business and in public administration. For a service firm, the process of developing a business model to improve performance will typically involve three steps (Sheehan and Stabell, 2007):

➤ *Step 1. Identifying the type of knowledge organization*: Key value-creating activities as a problem-solving organization; reputation capital that attracts cases to the organization; and governance of independence from police as well as interoperability with the police.

➤ *Step 2. Mapping the organization*: Opportunities and threats to police oversight; and strengths and weaknesses of the police oversight agency.

➤ *Step 3. Generating new business model*: New value creating activities; new assets; and new governance structure.

Stages of growth models have been used widely in both organizational research and information technology management research. According to King and Teo (1997), these models describe a wide variety of phenomena — the organizational life cycle, product life cycle, biological growth, and so forth. These models assume that predictable patterns (conceptualized in terms of stages) exist in the growth of organizations, the sales levels of products, the diffusion of information technology, and the growth of living organisms. These stages are (i) sequential in nature, (ii) occur as a hierarchical progression that is not easily reversed, and (iii) involve a broad range of organizational activities and structures. This is the core idea of the concept of growth models.

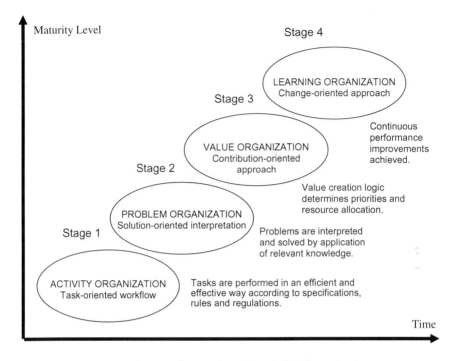

Figure 2.   Stages of Growth in Knowledge Organizations.

Figure 2 illustrates a potential stage model for knowledge organizations:

➢ Stage 1. *Activity Organization*. Tasks are performed and completed in workflows according to specifications, rules and regulations. It is important to avoid mistakes and delays in the workflows. Activity repetition and completion is measured and monitored. Management is concerned with resource allocation and utilization according to tasks to be completed. The organization structure is broken down into work groups according to division of labor.

➢ Stage 2. *Problem Organization*. Each new assignment is perceived more as a problem to be solved than as a task to be completed. Problems are interpreted and solved by application of relevant knowledge. The quality of problem solution is more important than workflow performance or resource utilization. Management is concerned with quality control so that the solution really solves the problem. Interoperability is important at this stage in terms of technical as well as semantic interoperability, where technical interoperability among knowledge workers ensures access to each other and semantic interoperability ensures shared understanding.

➢ Stage 3. *Value Organization*. Value creation logic determines priorities and resource allocation. The value that might be created by working on and solving a problem determines how each problem is perceived and understood. A value organization makes strategic decisions about the role of the organization as it relates to the specter of problems with which it is confronted. Performance goals are important at this stage, where goal setting is part of the strategy process, while goal achievement is part of the management process.

➢ Stage 4. *Learning Organization*. Continuous improvements are to be achieved based on experience. Change in resources, activities and approaches occur in the organization on a continuous basis. Communication channels are expanded internally (intra-organization) as well as externally (inter-organization). An organizational culture of sharing, transparency and contribution is stimulated. At this stage, supply-side knowledge management is replaced by demand-side knowledge management. Here, knowledge sources are familiar to everyone and knowledge sharing occurs on demand for that knowledge.

In knowledge organizations at Stage 4, transformational and charismatic leadership is an influential mode of leadership that is associated with high levels of individual and organizational performance. Leadership effectiveness is critically contingent on, and often defined in terms of, leaders' ability to motivate followers toward collective goals or a collective mission or vision (Kark and Dijk, 2007).

Knowledge Resources

Knowledge is a renewable, reusable and accumulating resource of value to the organization when applied in the production of products and services. Knowledge cannot as such be stored in computers; it can only be stored in the human brain. Knowledge is what a knower knows; there is no knowledge without someone knowing it.

The need for a knower in knowledge existence raises the question as to how knowledge can exist outside the heads of individuals. Although knowledge cannot originate outside the heads of individuals, it can be argued that knowledge can be represented in and often embedded in organizational processes, routines, and networks, and sometimes in document repositories. However, knowledge is seldom complete outside of an individual.

In this book, knowledge is defined as information combined with experience, context, interpretation, reflection, intuition and creativity. Information becomes knowledge once it is processed in the mind of an individual. This knowledge then becomes information again once it is articulated or communicated to others in the form of text, computer output, spoken, or written words or other means. Six characteristics of knowledge can distinguish it from information: knowledge is a human act, knowledge is the residue of thinking, knowledge is created in the present moment, knowledge belongs to communities, knowledge circulates through communities in many ways, and new knowledge is created at the boundaries of old. This definition and these characteristics of knowledge are based on current research (e.g., Poston and Speier, 2005; Wasko and Faraj, 2005).

Today, any discussion of knowledge quickly leads to the issue of how knowledge is defined. A pragmatic definition defines the topic as the most valuable form of content in a continuum starting at data, encompassing information, and ending at knowledge.

Typically, data are classified, summarized, transferred or corrected in order to add value, and become information within a certain context. This conversion is relatively mechanical and has long been facilitated by storage, processing, and communication technologies. These technologies add place, time, and form utility to the data. In doing so, the information serves to inform or reduce uncertainty within the problem domain. Therefore, information is united with the context, that is, it only has utility within the context.

Knowledge has the highest value, the most human contribution, the greatest relevance to decisions and actions, and the greatest dependence on a specific situation or context. It is also the most difficult of content types to manage, because it originates and is applied in the minds of human beings. People who are knowledgeable not only have information, but also have the ability to integrate and frame the information within the context of their experience, expertise, and judgment. In doing so, they can create new information that expands the state of possibilities, and in turn allows for further interaction with experience, expertise and judgment. Therefore, in an organizational context, all new knowledge stems from people. Some knowledge is incorporated in organizational artifacts like processes, structures, and technology. However, institutionalized knowledge often inhibits competition in a dynamic context, unless adaptability of people and processes (higher order learning) is built into the institutional mechanisms themselves.

Our concern with distinctions between information and knowledge is based on real differences as well as technology implications. Real differences between information and knowledge do exist, although for most practical purposes these differences are of no interest at all. Information technology implications are concerned with the argument that computers can only manipulate electronic information, not electronic knowledge. Business systems are loaded with information, but without knowledge.

Some have defined knowledge as a fluid mix of framed experience, values, contextual information, and expert insights that provides a framework for evaluating and incorporating new experiences and information. It originates and is applied in the mind of a knower. In organizations, it often becomes embedded not only in documents or repositories but also in organizational routines, processes, practices, and norms. Distinctions are often made between data, information, knowledge and wisdom:

Data are letters and numbers without meaning. Data are independent, isolated measurements, characters, numerical characters and symbols.

Information is data that are included in a context that makes sense. For example, 40 degrees can have different meaning depending on the context. There can be a medical, geographical or technical context. If a person has 40 degrees Celsius in fever, that is quite serious. If a city is located 40 degrees north, we know that it is far south of Norway. If an angle is 40 degrees, we know what it looks like. Information is data that make sense, because it can be understood correctly. People turn data into information by organizing it into some unit of analysis, e.g., dollars, dates, or customers. Information is data endowed with relevance and purpose.

Knowledge is information combined with experience, context, interpretation and reflection. Knowledge is a renewable resource that can be used over and over, and that accumulates in an organization through use and combination with employees' experience. Humans have knowledge; knowledge cannot exist outside the heads of individuals in the company. Information becomes knowledge when it enters the human brain. This knowledge transforms into information again when it is articulated and communicated to others. Information is an explicit representation of knowledge; it is in itself no knowledge. Knowledge can both be truths and lies, perspectives and concepts, judgments and expectations. Knowledge is used to receive information by analyzing, understanding and evaluating; by combining, prioritizing and decision making; and by planning, implementing and controlling.

Wisdom is knowledge combined with learning, insights and judgmental abilities. Wisdom is more difficult to explain than knowledge, since the levels of context become even more personal, and thus the higher-level nature of wisdom renders it more obscure than knowledge. While knowledge is mainly sufficiently generalized solutions, wisdom is best thought of as sufficiently generalized approaches and values that can be applied in numerous and varied situations. Wisdom cannot be created like data and information, and it cannot be shared with others like knowledge. Because the context is so personal, it becomes almost exclusive to our own minds and incompatible with the minds of others without extensive transaction. This transaction requires not only a base of knowledge and opportunities for experiences that help create wisdom, but also the processes of introspection, retrospection, interpretation and contemplation. We can value wisdom in others, but we can only create it ourselves.

It has been argued that expert systems using artificial intelligence are able to do knowledge work. The chess-playing computer called Deep Blue by IBM is frequently cited as an example. Deep Blue can compete with the best human players because chess, though complex, is a closed system of unchanging rules that are codified. The size of the board never varies, the rules are unambiguous, the moves of the pieces are clearly defined, and there is absolute agreement about what it means to win or lose. Deep Blue is no knowledge worker; the computer only performs a series of computations at extremely high speed.

While knowledge workers develop knowledge, organizations learn. Therefore, the learning organization has become a term frequently used. The learning organization is similar to knowledge development. While knowledge development is taking place at the individual level, organizational learning is taking place at the firm level. Organizational learning occurs when the firm is able to exploit individual competence in new and innovative ways. Organizational learning also occurs when the collective memory — including local language, common history and routines — expands. Organizational learning causes growth in the intellectual capital. Learning is a continuous, never-ending process of knowledge creation. A learning organization is a place where people are constantly driven to discover what has caused the current situation, and how they can change the present. To maintain competitive advantage, an organization's investment decisions related to knowledge creation are likely to be strategic in nature.

Our perspective of knowledge applied in this chapter is derived from the resource-based theory of the firm, as introduced in Chapter 1. According to the resource-based theory of the firm, performance differences across firms can be attributed to the variance in the firms' resources and capabilities. In this chapter, we focus on knowledge. Knowledge that is valuable, unique, difficult to imitate, combinable, difficult to substitute and exploitable can provide the basis for firms' competitive advantages. The essence of the resource-based theory of the firm lies in its emphasis on the internal resources — here knowledge — available to the firm, rather than on the external opportunities and threats dictated by industry conditions and market change.

Core Competence

According to Prahalad and Hamel (1990), core competencies are the collective learning in the organization, especially how to coordinate diverse service skills and integrate multiple streams of technologies. Since core competence is about harmonizing streams of technology, it is also about the organization of work and the delivery of value. Core competence does not diminish with use. Unlike physical assets, which do deteriorate over time, competencies are enhanced as they are applied and shared.

But competencies still need to be nurtured and protected; knowledge fades if it is not used. Competencies are the glue that binds existing business and coordinate service innovation. They are also the engines for new business development. At least three tests can be applied to identify core competencies in a company. First, a core competence provides potential access to a wide variety of markets. Second, a core competence should make a significant contribution to the perceived customer benefits of the end product. Finally, a core competence should be difficult for competitors to imitate.

The tangible link between identified core competencies and end products is what Prahalad and Hamel (1990) call core products — the embodiments of one or more core competencies. Core products are the components or subassemblies that actually contribute to the value of the end products. Core competencies are sometimes called firm-specific competencies, resource deployments, invisible assets, and distinctive competencies.

Quinn (1999) argues that core competencies are not products or "those things we do relatively well". They are those activities, usually intellectually based service activities or systems that the company performs better than any other enterprise. They are the sets of skills and systems that a company does at best-in-the-world levels and through which a company creates uniquely high value for customers. Developing best-in-the-world capabilities is crucial in designing a core competency strategy. Unless the company is best in the world at an activity, it is someone else's core competency. The company gives up competitive edge by not buying that skill from a best-in-the-world source.

Competence and capability are terms often used interchangeably (Madhavaram and Hunt, 2008). However, competence represents implicit and invisible assets, while capability represents an explicit knowledge set. Leonard-Barton (1992) adopted a knowledge-based view of the firm and defined core capability as the knowledge set that distinguishes and provides competitive advantage. There are four dimensions to this knowledge set. Its content is embodied in (1) employee knowledge and skills and embedded in (2) technical systems. The processes of knowledge creation and control are guided by (3) managerial systems. The fourth dimension is (4) the values and norms associated with the various types of embodied and embedded knowledge and with the processes of knowledge creation and control.

Harreld *et al.* (2007) suggest that capabilities build on the notion of competencies but focus on the role of management in building and adapting these competencies to address rapidly changing environments. Dynamic capabilities help enterprises to identify opportunities and mobilize competencies by reallocating resources. The ability to adapt and extend existing competencies is a key characteristic of dynamic capabilities. This ability places responsibility for entrepreneurship on executive management, as they must be able to accurately sense changes and opportunities. They must also act on these opportunities to be able to seize them by reconfiguring both tangible and intangible assets to meet new challenges.

Similar to core competencies, capabilities are considered core if they differentiate a company strategically. The concept is not new. Their strategic significance has been discussed for decades, stimulated by research discovery that of nine diversification strategies, the two that were built on an existing skill or resource base in the firm were associated with the highest performance. The observation that industry-specific capabilities increased the likelihood a firm could exploit a new technology within that industry, has confirmed the early work.

Therefore, some authors suggest that effective competition is based less on strategic leaps than on incremental innovation that exploits carefully developed capabilities. On the other hand, institutionalized capabilities may lead to incumbent inertia in the face of environmental changes. Technological discontinuities can enhance or destroy existing competencies within an industry. Such shifts in the external environment resonate within the organization, so that even seemingly minor innovations can undermine the usefulness of deeply embedded knowledge. All innovation necessarily requires some degree of creative destruction.

A capability is defined as dynamic if, in a rapidly changing environment, it enables the firm to modify itself so as to continue to produce, efficiently and/or effectively, market offerings for some market segments (Madhavaram and Hunt, 2008).

Entrepreneurship Capabilities

Corporate entrepreneurship is crucial in the acquisition of dynamic organizational capabilities (Zahra *et al.*, 1999). Scholars have identified entrepreneurship as the core process by which companies have attempted to redefine, renew, and remake themselves.

An entrepreneurship perspective on the nature of the firm rests on two fundamental assumptions about the nature of business activity: profit-seeking individuals and asymmetrically dispersed knowledge across economic actors. The quest for profit, wealth and power plays an important motivational role in the entrepreneur's pursuit of new business opportunities. Asymmetrically dispersed knowledge implies differentiated sets of knowledge held by decision makers, which in the business context causes variation in the ability to identify and assimilate new information and events. Individual decision makers tend to notice new information that relates to and can be combined with knowledge they already have (Zander, 2007).

An entrepreneur is a person who operates a new enterprise or venture or revitalizes an existing enterprise and assumes some accountability for the inherent risk. The new and modern view on the entrepreneurial talent is that of a person who takes the risks involved to undertake a business venture. Entrepreneurship is often difficult and tricky, as many new ventures fail. In the context of the creation of for-profit enterprises, "entrepreneur" is often synonymous with "founder". Most commonly, the term "entrepreneur" applies to someone who creates value by offering a product or service in order to obtain certain profit.

Entrepreneurship is thus the practice of starting new organizations or revitalizing mature organizations, particularly new businesses, generally in response to identified opportunities. Entrepreneurship is sometimes labeled entrepreneurialism. Entrepreneurship is often a difficult undertaking, as a vast majority of new businesses fail. Entrepreneurial activity is substantially different from operational activity as it is mainly concerned with creativity and innovation. Entrepreneurship ranges from small individual initiatives to major undertakings creating many job opportunities.

The majority of recent theories in the business and managerial economic literature assume that the economic performance of small and medium-sized firms depends largely on the entrepreneurs' (or team's) capacities. Even so, economists still do not fully understand the relationship between entrepreneurs and firm performance. The entrepreneurial process is the result of a complex interaction between individual, social and environmental factors. Taken separately, neither the personality of the entrepreneur nor the structural characteristics of the environment can, on its own, determine an organization's performance (Thomas and Mancino, 2007).

In order to provide an example of the relationship between entrepreneurs' subjective characteristics/traits and organizational performance, Thomas and Mancino (2007) carried out an empirical study. The study aimed to explain how the presence of entrepreneurs' specific subjective characteristics can influence an organization's strategic orientation and, as a consequence, local development. By analyzing several subjective characteristics taken from a sample of 101 successful entrepreneurs from southern Italy, certain issues emerged regarding the link between the economic performance of the ventures launched in this area and the weak level of growth. Successful entrepreneurs' behavior and decisions seemed heavily influenced by family support. The entrepreneurial culture of the family also tends to substitute the protective role played by public institutions. The entrepreneurial decisions of local entrepreneurs are triggered both by their need to rid themselves of poverty and their feeling that they are destined to continue the family business, the majority of them being the children of entrepreneurs. Most of the interviewees were classified as necessity rather than opportunity entrepreneurs.

An entrepreneur might be driven by a compulsive need to find new ways of allocating resources. He or she might be searching for profit-making opportunities and engineer incremental changes in products and processes. While strongly innovative entrepreneurs tend to champion radical changes in resource allocation by making new service markets and pioneering new processes, weakly innovative entrepreneurs tend to seek small changes in resource allocation to explore profit-making opportunities between already established activities (Markovski and Hall, 2007).

Founders of new legal firms tend to be experienced professionals who pursue opportunities closely related to their previous employment. Entrepreneurs often have several years of work experience in the same industry as their own start-up enterprises. This suggests that entrepreneurs do not come from out of the blue, but build their human intellectual capital through work experience in established firms. Similarly, criminal entrepreneurs might be experienced professionals before establishing their own criminal business enterprise.

A Case of Dynamic Capabilities

So far in this chapter, we have explained the definitions and relationships of knowledge, skills, capabilities, organizational capabilities and core competencies as they relate to the resource-based and knowledge-based theory of the firm. Next, we will exemplify the concepts of dynamic capabilities exhibited by agile organizations, as they relate to dynamic knowledge management and the practice of excellent strategy execution.

Harreld *et al.* (2007) present the case of dynamic capabilities at IBM. They argue that dynamic capabilities are driving strategy into action in the firm. They studied the rise, fall, and transformation of IBM during a 20-year period. IBM's dynamic capabilities transformed IBM from a set of conventional silos (e.g., hardware, software, and services) to an integrated structure oriented to provide solutions for customer needs. To make this new approach work, the entire role of the corporate strategy group at IBM needed to change.

Dynamic capabilities enable the sensing of changes in a competitive environment as well as the seizure of opportunities. To ensure that the strategy process at IBM provides the insight necessary to sense opportunities and the execution required to seize them, a set of complementary mechanisms have evolved. Strategic leadership forums and other initiatives help explore into new spaces, while metrics and structure help exploit existing capabilities and processes.

Sensing new opportunities to gain strategic insight is conducted in a number of processes at IBM (Harreld *et al.*, 2007):

➢ The Technology Team meets monthly and assesses the market readiness and the potential of emerging technologies.
➢ The Strategy Team meets monthly to examine the market results of existing unit strategies as well as to explore new growth areas.
➢ The Integration and Value Team meets quarterly to support company-wide initiatives.
➢ Deep Dive processes are initiated when confronting a performance or opportunity gap to scrutinize a topic in great detail.

Each of these processes help ensure steady surveillance and intelligence of the competitive environment. Intelligence is the systematic approach to collecting information with the purpose of tracking and predicting change to improve business performance. Intelligence analysts investigate who are the actors, how, when, where and why. They provide recommendations on how to react to market changes and opportunities. As part of this, analysts may produce profiles of market problems and targets, and produce both strategic (overall, long-term) and tactical (specific, short-term) assessments within the confines set by the business and the industry.

Seizing new opportunities for strategic execution is conducted in a number of processes at IBM (Harreld *et al.*, 2007):

• Emerging Business Opportunities are an integrated set of processes, incentives, and structures designed explicitly to enable

IBM to address new business opportunities and drive revenue growth.

- Strategic Leadership Forums are several days of team-based workshops built around specific performance or opportunity gaps that bring extended teams together for intensive work on problems or opportunities.
- Corporate Investment Funds are a way of providing funding for new initiatives identified by the Integration and Value Teams.

Harreld *et al.* (2007) argue that unlike other piecemeal approaches to strategy, the IBM process is one driven by line management based on the realities of the marketplace as seen in performance or opportunities gaps, not a staff exercise or slide deck. This has moved the strategy-making process from an annual ritual to a continual process, from an emphasis on planning to one on action, from a staff function to one that line managers own, and from a concern with strategy only to a focus on both strategy and execution.

Knowledge Driven Innovation

Knowledge resources, core competencies and dynamic capabilities are key drivers of service innovation in firms. Based on such drivers, a variety of modes of innovation emerge in knowledge-intensive business services. For example, Corrocher *et al.* (2009) identified the interactive innovation mode, the techno-organizational mode, the conservative mode, and the product innovation mode for knowledge-intensive business services:

- The interactive innovation mode occurs in the interaction with other firms and customers.
- The techno-organizational mode occurs when technology adoption is not an isolated and passive strategy, but is closely intertwined with changes associated with the way in which services are provided and organized.

- The conservative mode occurs when a firm does not carry out any relevant innovation activity.
- The product innovation mode occurs when innovative ideas are linked to manufacturing.

Corrocher *et al.* (2009) found that the attention paid to the innovative activities of service sectors has significantly increased over the last decade. Simultaneity of production and consumption and the intangible nature of the service make long distance trade more difficult than for goods and give a local flavor to competition, even when considering the more sophisticated services. This is particularly evident in advanced regions, where competitiveness depends on knowledge content, provided by highly specialized experts.

Therefore, knowledge production is increasingly directed at business services. The emphasis is laid in the role of business services in innovative networks as carriers of knowledge and intermediates between science (knowledge creator) and their customers (knowledge users). An empirical analysis by Hipp (1999) shows that knowledge-intensive business services are able to make existing knowledge useful for their customers, improving the customer's performance and productivity and contributing to technological and structural change.

In this context, knowledge-intensive business services are defined in terms of service characteristics and knowledge characteristics. Among service characteristics we find close interaction between service provider and customer and highly intangible content of service products and processes. Among knowledge characteristics we find ability to receive information from outside the firm and to transform this information together with firm-specific knowledge into useful services for their customers (Hipp, 1999).

Madhavaram and Hunt (2008) argue there is a service-dominant logic in resource management. They apply resource-advantage theory to suggest marketing's evolution toward a new dominant logic that requires the focus of marketing to be on the intangible, dynamic, operant resources that are the heart of competitive advantage and performance.

Drawing from the resources, competencies, resource-advantage theory, capabilities, and dynamic capabilities literature, Madhavaram and Hunt (2008) extend and elaborate on the service-dominant logic's notion of operant resources by proposing a hierarchy of operant resources. Starting from the seven basic resource categories (financial, physical, legal, human, organizational, informational, and relational), they propose basic, composite, and interconnected operant resources as the hierarchy.

Innovation in services very often includes creative application of information technology found in the technological dimension of innovation. However, as pointed out by Gallouj and Savona (2009), innovation in services is becoming an increasingly complex issue, in which the adoption of information and communications technology is just one of many possible facilitators.

A number of important concepts have been introduced in this chapter, including knowledge, knowledge management, core competencies, and dynamic capabilities. These concepts represent perspectives to gain insights into barriers and enablers of service innovation. At the center of these concepts we find knowledge as a resource to be explored and exploited for the benefit of innovation in services.

Chapter 10
Intelligence Strategy

An intelligence strategy is needed for business intelligence. As mentioned in chapter 9, business intelligence is a process of taking large amounts of data, analyzing that data, and presenting a high-level set of reports that condense the essence of that data into the basis of business actions. Business intelligence can enable management to gain new insights and thereby contributing to their business decisions to prevent white-collar crime and to strengthen corporate reputation.

Strategy Characteristics

Traditionally, intelligence was understood to mean information from criminals about criminal activity by a covert source. Today, intelligence is a systematic approach to collecting information with the purpose, for example, of tracking and predicting crime to improve law enforcement (Brown *et al.*, 2004).

The aim of intelligence strategy is to continue to develop intelligence-led policing in all parts of an organization, a nation or in all regions of the world. An intelligence strategy provides a framework for a structured problem-solving and partnership-enhanced approach, based around a common model. For example, the National Intelligence Model in the UK is a structured approach to improve intelligence-led policing both centrally and locally in policing districts such as the South Yorkshire Police (SYPIS, 2007).

Intelligence-led policing is carried out in many law enforcement areas. For example, intelligence-led vehicle crime reduction was carried out in the West Surrey police area in the UK. Analysis of vehicle crime included identifying (Brown *et al.*, 2004):

1. Locations (hotspots, streets, car parks, postcodes, wards, etc.) of vehicle crime,
2. Sites where vehicles were dumped,
3. Times of offences,
4. Prolific vehicle crime offenders,
5. Areas where prolific offenders were identified as offending,
6. Models of vehicles targeted for vehicle crime,
7. Type of property stolen in theft from vehicle offences.

The analysis resulted in problem profiles, which identified emerging patterns of crime. These patterns included vehicle crime occurring in beauty spot car parks and the theft of badges from cars. Such information was disseminated to local officers to act on.

Intelligence-led policing is defined as a business model and a management philosophy according to Ratcliffe (2008: 89):

> Intelligence-led policing is a business model and managerial philosophy where data analysis and crime intelligence are pivotal to an objective, decision-making framework that facilitates crime and problem reduction, disruption and prevention through both strategic management and effective enforcement strategies that target prolific and serious offenders.

An interesting case of intelligence-led policing in the UK was the project called "Operation Gallant" that lead to a reduction of 17% in car thefts. Operation Gallant involved all officers in a Basic Command Unit (BCU) in the collection and analysis of information (Brown *et al.*, 2004: 2):

> In the case of Operation Gallant, the intelligence-led vehicle crime reduction approach involved the activity of officers from across a BCU. A crime analyst, dedicated solely to examine vehicle crime patterns and trends, developed a detailed picture of vehicle crime in the area, including analysis of time, location, vehicle type and known offenders. As a result of this strategic analysis, a number of interventions were planned, drawing heavily upon the Operation Igneous tactical menu. The most significant, in terms of resources

devoted to the operation, involved a program of prolific offender targeting and crime prevention advice targeted towards the owners of high-risk vehicles.

The substantial decline in car crimes were explained by the increased attention paid to this crime sector (Brown *et al.*, 2004: 16):

> Given the fact that the first reduction coincides with the commencement of the planning process for Operation Gallant, this may also reflect an anticipatory effect in which the very act of planning and talking about an operation leads to a decline.

Information Sources

In intelligence work for investigating and preventing white-collar crime, a variety of information sources are available. Sheptycki (2007) lists the following information sources in policing for general corporate social responsibility work: victim reports, witness reports, police reports, crime scene examinations, historical data held by police agencies (such as criminal records), prisoner debriefings, technical or human surveillance products, suspicious financial transactions reporting, and reports emanating from undercover police operations. Similarly, internal investigation units in business organizations can apply intelligence sources. Intelligence analysis may also refer to governmental records of other governmental departments and agencies, and other more open sources of information may be used in elaborate intelligence assessment. Most of the information used to prevent and investigate financial crime is sensitive, complex, and the result of time consuming tasks (Wilhelmsen, 2009).

However, Sheptycki (2007) found that most crime analysis is organized around existing investigation and prevention sector data. Intelligence analysis is typically framed by already existing institutional ways of thinking. He argues that organized crime notification, classification and measurement schemes tend to reify pre-existing notions of traditional policing practice.

In this perspective, it is important for strategic criminal analysts to be aware of the variety of information sources available. We choose to classify information sources into the following categories in this book:

1. *Interview.* By means of *interrogation* of witnesses, suspects, reference persons and experts, information is collected on crimes, criminals, times and places, organizations, criminal projects, activities, roles, etc.
2. *Network.* By means of *informants* in the criminal underworld as well as in legal businesses, information is collected on actors, plans, competitors, markets, customers, etc. Informants often have connections with persons that an investigating colleague would not be able to approach formally.
3. *Location.* By analyzing potential and actual *crime scenes* and potential criminal scenes, information is collected on criminal procedures, preferences, crime evolution, etc. Hot spots and traces are found. Secret ransacking of suspicious places is part of this information source. Pictures in terms of crime scene photographs are important information elements.
4. *Documents.* Studying documents from *confiscations* may provide information on ownership, transactions, accounts, etc. An example is forensic accounting, which is the application of accounting tasks for an evidentiary purpose. Forensic accounting is the action of identifying, recording, settling, extracting, sorting, reporting and verifying past financial data or other accounting activities for settling current or prospective legal disputes or using such past financial data for projecting future financial data to settle legal disputes. Forensic accountants are essential to the legal system, providing expert services such as fake invoicing valuations, suspicious bankruptcy valuations, and analysis of financial documents in fraud schemes (Curtis, 2008).
5. *Observation.* By means of *anonymous personal presence*, both individuals and activities can be observed. Both in the physical and the virtual world, observation is important in financial crime intelligence. An example is digital forensics, where successful

cyber crime intelligence requires computer skills and modern systems in policing. Digital forensics is the art and science of applying computer science to aid the legal process. It is more than the technological, systematic inspection of electronic systems and their contents for evidence or supportive evidence of a criminal act. Digital forensics requires specialized expertise and tools when applied to intelligence in important areas such as online victimization of children.

6. *Action.* For example, *provocation* is an action by the investigating unit to cause reactions that represents intelligence information. In the case of online victimization of children, online grooming offenders in a pedophile ring are identified and their reaction to provocations leads intelligence officers into new nodes (persons, computers) and new actual and potential victims. While the individual pedophile is mainly concerned with combining indecent image impression and personal fantasy to achieve personal satisfaction, online organizers of sexual abuse of children are doing it for profit. By claiming on the Internet to be a boy or girl of 9 years, police provoke contact with criminal business enterprises making money on pedophile customers. Undercover operations by police officers do belong to the action category of information sources as well.

7. *Surveillance.* Surveillance of places by means of *video cameras* as well as microphones for viewing and listening belong to this information source. Many business organizations have surveillance cameras on their premises to control entrants and other critical areas. It is possible for the police to be listening in on what is discussed in a room without the participants knowing. For example, police in a country identified which room was used by local Hells Angels members in their resort for crime planning and installed listening devices in that room. Harfield (2008: 64) argues that when surveillance is employed to produce evidence, such product is often considered incontrovertible (hence defense lawyers' focus on process rather than

product when cross-examining surveillance officers): "An essentially covert activity, by definition, surveillance lacks transparency and is therefore vulnerable to abuse by over-zealous investigators".

8. *Communication control.* Wire tapping in terms of *interception* belongs to this category of information source. Police is listening in on what is discussed on a telephone or data line without the participants knowing. In the UK, the interception of communications (telephone calls, emails, letters, etc.), whilst generating intelligence to identify more conventional evidential opportunities, is excluded from trial evidence by law, to the evident incredulity of foreign law enforcement colleagues (Harfield, 2008).

9. *Physical material.* Investigation of material to identify for example *fingerprints* on doors or bags, or material to identify blood type from blood splatters. Another example is legal visitation, which is an approach to identify illegal material. DNA is emerging as an important information source, where DNA is derived from physical material such as hair or spit from a person. Police search is one approach to physical material collection.

10. *Internet.* As an *open source,* the Internet is as important for general information and specific happenings to corporate crime intelligence as to everyone else. It is important to note that use of open sources is not at all a new activity and not a new phenomenon of the Internet, which is not in itself a source, but a tool at finding sources. Also, there are risks of using open sources such as self-corroboration.

11. *Policing systems.* Readily available in most police agencies are *police records.* For example, DNA records may prove helpful when having DNA material from new suspects. Similarly, corporate social responsibility units may develop records that do not violate privacy rights.

12. *Employees.* Information from the *local community* is often supplied as tips to local police using law enforcement tip lines.

Similarly, a corporate social responsibility unit is receiving tips from employees in various departments.

13. *Accusations*. Victimized persons and goods file a *claim* with the corporate investigation unit or the unit for corporate social responsibility.

14. *Exchange*. International *policing cooperation* includes exchange of intelligence information. International partners for national police include national police in other countries as well as multinational organizations such as Europol and Interpol. Similarly, trade organizations and other entities for business organizations create exchanges for financial crime intelligence.

15. *Media*. By reading newspapers and watching TV, intelligence officers get access to *news*.

16. *Control authorities*. Cartel agencies, stock exchanges, tax authorities and other control authorities are *suppliers of information* to the corporate executives in case of suspicious transactions.

17. *External data storage*. A number of business and government organizations store information that may be useful in financial crime intelligence. For example, telecom firms store data about traffic, where both sender and receiver are registered with date and time of communication.

All these information sources have different characteristics. For example, information sources can be distinguished in terms of the extent of trustworthiness and the extent of accessibility.

Prisons and other correctional environments are potential places for several information sources and production of intelligence useful to law enforcement. The total prison environment, including the physical plant, the schedule regimens of both staff and inmates, and all points of ingress and egress can be legitimately tapped for intelligence purposes in countries such as the US (Maghan, 1994). Since organized criminals often are sophisticated in using the correction environment to their advantage, police and correction personnel need immersion in the intelligence operations and strategies of their respective agencies. Legal visitation and escape attempts are sources of information. Prisoners are reluctant to testify, and their credibility is easily attacked. Communication control is derived from inmate use of phones, visits, mail, and other contacts.

The 17 information sources can be classified into two main categories. The first category includes all person-oriented information sources, where the challenge in corporate intelligence is to communicate with individuals. The second category includes all media-oriented information sources, where the challenge in corporate intelligence is to manage and use different technological and other media. This distinction into two main categories leads to the following classification of the 17 information sources:

A. *Person-oriented information sources*

1. Interrogation in interview
2. Informants in network
5. Anonymous, individual presence undercover for observation
6. Provocation through action
12. Tips from citizens in local community
13. Claims in accusations
14. Information exchange in inter-organizational cooperation

B. *Media-oriented information sources*

3. Crime scenes at location
4. Confiscated documents
7. Video cameras for surveillance
8. Interception for communication control
9. Physical materials such as fingerprints
10. Open sources such as Internet
11. Internal records in policing systems
15. News in the media
16. Supply of information from control authorities
17. External data storage

Combinations of information sources are selected in investigation and intelligence depending on the subject of white-collar crime. When forensic accounting is applied as document study, it is typically combined with interviews and observations, thereby integrating behavioral aspects into forensic accounting (Ramamoorti, 2008).

Knowledge Categories

Information sources provide the raw material for knowledge work to prevent white-collar crime and strengthen corporate reputation. Knowledge has to be identified in terms of categories and levels. One identification approach suggested here is the knowledge matrix approach. A knowledge matrix is a table that lists knowledge needs. The matrix shows knowledge categories and knowledge levels.

Here we make distinctions between the following knowledge categories for investigating and preventing financial crime:

1. *Administrative knowledge* is knowledge about the role of management and executive leadership. It is knowledge about procedures, rules and regulations.
2. *Organization knowledge* is knowledge about how the business is organized and management as a law enforcement role. This is knowledge at the organizational level.
3. *Employee knowledge* is knowledge about where employees spend their working hours, what they do, and why they do it. This is knowledge at the individual level.
4. *Process knowledge* is knowledge about work processes and practices in business work when committing financial crime. Process knowledge is based on police science, which includes all aspects of policing internally as well as externally (Jaschke *et al.*, 2007). It includes external factors that influence the role and behavior of policing in society.
5. *Investigative knowledge* is knowledge based on case-specific and case-oriented collection of information to confirm or disconfirm whether an act or no-act is criminal. Included here are case

documents and evidence in such a form that they prove useful in a court case.

6. *Intelligence knowledge* is knowledge based on a systematic collection of information concerned with a certain topic, a certain domain, certain persons or any other focused scope. Collected information is transformed and processed according to a transparent methodology to discover criminal capacity, dispositions and goals. Transformation and processing generate new insights into criminality that guide the effectiveness and efficiency of prevention and investigation. Included in intelligence knowledge is phenomenological knowledge, which is defined as knowledge about a phenomenon, in terms of what it is about (know-what), how it works (know-how), and why it works (know-why). Phenomenological knowledge enables intelligence workers to "see" what "something" is about, by understanding and not information when overlooking it emerges.

7. *Legal knowledge* is knowledge of the law, regulations and legal procedures. It is based on access to a variety of legal sources, both nationally and internationally, including court decisions. Legal knowledge is composed of declarative, procedural and analytical knowledge. Declarative knowledge is law and other regulations. Procedural knowledge is the practice of law. Analytical knowledge is the link between case information and laws.

8. *Technological knowledge* is knowledge about the development, use, exploitation and exploration of information and communication technology. It is knowledge about applications, systems, networks and databases.

9. *Analytical knowledge* is knowledge about the strategies, tactics and actions that executive managers and investigators can implement to reach desired goals.

In addition to the above classification into knowledge categories, we also make distinctions between knowledge levels:

➢ *Basic knowledge* is knowledge necessary to get work done. Basic knowledge is required for an intelligence officer and investigator as a knowledge worker to understand and interpret information, and basic knowledge is required for an intelligence and investigation unit as a knowledge organization to receive input and produce output. However, basic knowledge alone produces only elementary and basic results of little value and low quality.

➢ *Advanced knowledge* is knowledge necessary to get good work done. Advanced knowledge is required for an intelligence officer and investigator as a knowledge worker to achieve satisfactory work performance, and advanced knowledge is required for an intelligence and investigation unit as a knowledge organization to produce intelligence reports and crime analysis as well as charges that are useful in investigation and prevention of financial crime. When advanced knowledge is combined with basic knowledge, then we find professional knowledge workers and professional knowledge organizations in law enforcement.

➢ *Innovative knowledge* is knowledge that makes a real difference. When intelligence officers and investigators apply innovative knowledge in intelligence and analysis of incoming and available information, then new insights are generated in terms of crime patterns, criminal profiles and prevention and investigation strategies. When intelligence units apply innovative knowledge, then new methodologies in intelligence and analysis are introduced, that corporate management can learn.

Based on these categories and levels, our knowledge matrix consists of 9 knowledge categories and 3 knowledge levels as illustrated in Table 1. The purpose of the table is to illustrate that there are a total of twenty-seven knowledge-needs in investigating and preventing financial crime. Based on the table, each intelligence unit and investigation unit has to identify and fill in the table for knowledge needs.

Knowledge levels were defined in Table 1 at basic knowledge, advanced knowledge and innovative knowledge. An alternative approach is to define knowledge levels in terms of knowledge

Table 1.   Knowledge Management Matrix for Knowledge Needs in Investigation and Prevention of Financial Crime in Organizations

#	Category	Basic Knowledge	Advanced Knowledge	Innovative Knowledge
1	Administrative knowledge	*The role of a complaints and whistle-blowing investigator*	*Sources of information*	*Best practice in complaints and crime investigations*
2	Organization knowledge	*How the business is organized and managed*	*How internal misconduct and crime is solved*	*Power structures in the organization and links to the criminal world*
3	Employee knowledge	*Where employees spend their working hours*	*What employees do in their working hours*	*Why employees do what they do in their working hours*
4	Process knowledge	*Information sources in investigation and prevention*	*Analyses techniques in investigation and prevention*	*Behavior in investigative and preventive work*
5	Investigative Knowledge	*Investigative procedures*	*Contingent approaches to investigations*	*Hypothesis and causality in crime*
6	Intelligence knowledge	*Intelligence procedures*	*Contingent approaches to intelligence*	*Hypotheses and causality in potential crime*
7	Legal knowledge	*What investigators can do*	*What investigators cannot do*	*Expected outcome of court procedure*
8	Technological knowledge	*Equipment in investigative work*	*Equipment in analysis work*	*Artificial intelligence and expert systems*
9	Analytical knowledge	*Analytical methods*	*Analytical procedures*	*Analytical creativity*

depth: know-what, know-how and know-why, as shown in Table 2. These knowledge depth levels represent the extent of insight and understanding about a phenomenon. While know-what is simple perception of what is going on, know-why is complicated insight

Table 2.   Alternative Knowledge Management Matrix for Knowledge Needs in Investigation and Prevention of Financial Crime in Organizations

#	Category	Know-What	Know-How	Know-Why
1	Administrative knowledge	*What investigating colleagues is all about*	*How investigating colleagues is done*	*Why investigation and prevention of financial crime is carried out*
2	Organization knowledge	*What employees do*	*How employees do the things they do*	*Why employees do the things they do*
3	Employee knowledge	*What colleagues do during their working hours*	*How colleagues do their work*	*Why colleagues do what they do*
4	Process knowledge	*What kinds of financial crime do occur*	*How financial crime does occur*	*Why financial crime does occur*
5	Investigative knowledge	*What investigative procedures are available*	*How investigative procedures work*	*Why investigative procedures work the way they do*
6	Intelligence knowledge	*What intelligence procedures are available*	*How intelligence procedures work*	*Why investigative procedures work the way they do*
7	Legal knowledge	*What laws and regulations are relevant for financial crime*	*How these laws and regulations are relevant for financial crime*	*Why these laws and regulations are relevant for financial crime*
8	Technological knowledge	*What technological means are available to enforce law on criminal employees*	*How these technological means enable law enforcement*	*Why these technological means enable law enforcement*
9	Analytical knowledge	*What approaches are successful in enforcing law on criminal employees*	*How these approaches are successful*	*Why these approaches are successful*

into cause-and-effect relationships in terms of why it is going on:

- ➢ *Know-what* is knowledge about what is happening and what is going on. An executive perceives that something is going on that might need his or her attention. The executive's insight is limited to perception of something happening. The executive neither understands how it is happening nor why it is happening.
- ➢ *Know-how* is knowledge about how financial crime develops, how a criminal behaves or how a criminal activity is organized. The executive's or investigator's insight is not limited to a perception of something that is happening; he or she also understands how it is happening or how it is.
- ➢ *Know-why* is the knowledge representing the deepest form of understanding and insight into a phenomenon. The executive or investigator does not only know that it occurs and how it occurs. He or she has also developed an understanding of why it occurs or why it is like this. Developing hypotheses about cause-and-effect relationships and empirically validating causality are important characteristics of know-why knowledge.

One part of the knowledge work is to investigate a crime where a colleague is a suspect. That type of internal policing is described above. It seems easy to forget another part of internal policing as well. It is not just executives, but also other colleagues who have a responsibility to prevent one another from getting involved in illegal actions during the business work. To succeed with that, executives and colleagues need knowledge mentioned above, and it is also important that internal police officers have an interest and dare to take action to prevent or react on illegal actions when taken by colleagues during work processes.

Value Shop Configuration

Investigation and prevention of white-collar crime and building corporate reputation have the value configuration of a value shop.

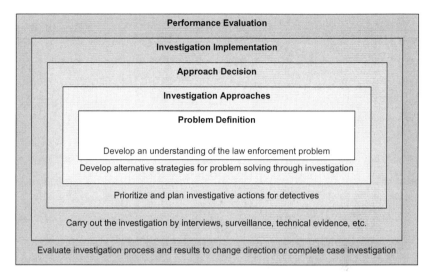

Figure 1.   The Knowledge Organization of Investigation and Prevention Units as Value Shop Activities.

As can be seen in Figure 1, the five activities of a value shop are interlocking and while they follow a logical sequence, much like the management of any project, the difference from a knowledge management perspective is the way in which knowledge is used as a resource to create value in terms of results for the organization. Hence, the logic of the five interlocking value shop activities in this example is of a policing unit and how it engages in its core business of conducting reactive and proactive investigations.

The sequence of activities starts with problem understanding, moves into alternative investigation approaches, investigation decision, and investigation implementation, and ends up with criminal investigation evaluation (Sheehan and Stabell, 2007). However, these five sequential activities tend to overlap and link back to earlier activities, especially in relation to activity 5 (control and evaluation) in policing units when the need for control and command structures are a daily necessity because of the legal obligations that policing unit authority entails. Hence, the diagram is meant to illustrate the reiterative and cyclical nature of these five primary activities for managing the knowledge collected during and applied to a specific investigation in a value shop manner.

Furthermore, Figure 1 illustrates the expanding domain of the knowledge work performed in financial crime investigations, starting in the centre with problem understanding and ending at the edge with evaluation of all parts of the investigation process.

These five primary activities of the value shop in relation to a financial crime investigation and prevention unit can be outlined as (Sheehan and Stabell, 2007):

1. *Problem Definition*. This involves working with parties to determine the exact nature of the crime and hence how it will be defined. For example, a physical assault in a domestic violence situation depending on how the responding officers choose and/or perceive to define it can be either upgraded to the status of grievous bodily harm to the female spouse victim or it may be downgraded to a less serious common, garden variety assault where a bit of rough handing took place towards the spouse. This concept of making crime, a term used on how detectives choose to make incidents into a crime or not, is highly relevant here and is why this first activity has been changed from the original problem finding term used in the business management realm to a problem definition process here in relation to policing work. Moreover, this first investigative activity involves deciding on the overall investigative approach for the case not only in terms of information acquisition but also as indicated in Figure 1, in undertaking the key task, usually by a senior investigative officer in a serious or major incident, of forming an appropriate investigative team to handle the case.

2. *Investigation Approaches*. This second activity of identifying problem-solving approaches involves the actual generation of ideas and action plans for the investigation. As such, it is a key process for it sets the direction and tone of the investigation and is very much influenced by the composition of the members of the

investigative team. For example, the experience level of investigators and their preferred investigative thinking style might be a critical success factor in this second primary activity of the value shop.

3. *Approach Decision.* This solution choice activity represents the decision of choosing between alternatives generated in the second activity. While the least important primary activity of the value shop in terms of time and effort, it might be the most important in terms of value. In this case, trying to ensure as far as is possible that what is decided on to do is the best option to follow to get an effective investigative result. A successful solution choice is dependent on two requirements. First, alternative investigation steps were identified in the problem-solving approaches activity. It is important to think in terms of alternatives. Otherwise, no choices can be made. Next, criteria for decision making have to be known and applied to the specific investigation.

4. *Investigation Implementation.* As the name implies, solution execution represents communicating, organizing, investigating, and implementing decisions. This is an equally important process or phase in an investigation as it involves sorting out from the mass of information coming into the incident room about a case and directing the lines of enquiry as well as establishing the criteria used to eliminate a possible suspect from further scrutiny in the investigation. A miscalculation here can stall or even ruin the whole investigation. Most of the resources spent on an investigation are used here in this fourth activity of the value shop.

5. *Performance Evaluation.* Control and evaluation involves monitoring activities and the measurement of how well the solution solved the original problem or met the original need. This is where the command and control chain of authority comes into play for investigation and prevention units and where the determination of the quality and quantity of the evidence is made as to whether or not to charge and prosecute an identified offender in a court of law.

Conclusion

White-collar crime represents a serious threat to corporate reputation. Nevertheless, there are surprisingly many corporations that are involved in white-collar crime. For example in Sweden, Alalehto (2010) found that 40 percent of the top-ranked corporations in the Swedish business world have been involved in white-collar crime in the last decade. These corporations had decisions against them, such as court decisions, administrative law, objection, or settlement.

Efficient and effective corporate governance and commitment to corporate social responsibility are elements that can prevent damage to corporate reputation and help rebuild corporate reputation after white-collar scandals. In addition, professional investigations have to be carried out on suspicion and intelligence has to be applied to cause red flags when relevant.

As argued by Avram and Kühne (2008), stressing the notion of responsible business behavior is not a matter of getting companies to move away from their usual way of doing business. Rather, responsible business behavior constitutes the consciousness that a company can do well in the long run by paying attention to the environment and the society in which it operates. Many of the pressing social and environmental problems are caused and can be solved by companies.

References

Abdolmohammadi, M.J. and Read, W.J. (2010). Corporate Governance Ratings and Financial Restatements: Pre and Post Sarbanes-Oxley Act, *Journal of Forensic & Investigative Accounting*, 2 (1), 1–44, www.bus.lsu.edu/accounting/faculty/lcrumbley/jfia/Articles.htm.

Abramova, I. (2007). The funding of traditional organized crime in Russia. *Economic Affairs*, 27 (1), 18–21.

Acquaah-Gaisie, G. (2000). Fighting public officer and corporate crimes, *Journal of Financial Crime*, 8 (1), 12–20.

Alalehto, T. (2010). The wealthy white-collar criminals: corporations as offenders, *Journal of Financial Crime*, 17 (3), 308–320.

Aldama, L.R.P., Amar, P.A. and Trostianki, D.W. (2009). Embedding corporate responsibility through effective organizational structure, *Corporate Governance*, 9 (4), 506–516.

Ariail, D.L., Blair, J.P. and Smith, L.M. (2010). Audit Inquiries and Deception Detection: Standards, Research, and Guidance, *Journal of Forensic & Investigative Accounting*, 2 (1), 1–25, www.bus.lsu.edu/accounting/faculty/lcrumbley/jfia/Articles. htm.

Ashforth, B.E., Gioia, D.A., Robinson, S.L. and Trevino, L.K. (2008). Re-reviewing organizational corruption, *The Academy of Management Review*, 33 (3), 670–684.

Attanasio, M.A. (2008). Handling criminal investigations, *Financial Executive*, December, 56–58.

Avram, D.O. and Kühne, S. (2008). Implementing responsible business behavior from a strategic management perspective: developing a framework for Austrian SMEs, *Journal of Business Ethics*, 82, 463–475.

Baer, M.H. (2008). Corporate policing and corporate governance: what can we learn from Hewlett-Packard's pretexting scandal? *New York University Public Law and Legal Theory Working Papers, Paper 73*, New York University School of Law, NY. http://lsr.nellco.org/nyn-plltwp/73/.

Baird, J.E. and Zelin, R.C. (2009). An examination of the impact of obedience pressure on perceptions of fraudulent acts and the likelihood of committing occupational fraud, *Journal of Forensic Studies in Accounting and Business*, Winter, 1–14.

Basu, K. and Palazzo, G. (2008). Corporate social responsibility: a process model of sensemaking, *Academy of Management Review*, 33 (1), 122–136.

Becht, M., Bolton, P. and Röell, A. (2007). Corporate law and governance, in *Handbook of Law and Economics*, Polinsky, A.M. and Shavell, S. (eds.) Amsterdam: Elsevier Publishing.

Benbasat, I., Dexter, A.S., Drury, D.H., Goldstein, R.H. (1984). A critique of the stage hypothesis: theory and empirical evidence. *Communications of the ACM*, 27 (5), 476–485.

Bennet, A. and Bennet, D. (2005a). Designing the Knowledge Organization of the Future: The Intelligent Complex Adaptive System, in *Handbook of Knowledge Management*, Holsapple, C.W. (ed.), Vol. 2, pp. 623–638. Netherlands: Springer Science & Business Media.

Bennet, D. and Bennet, A. (2005b). The Rise of the Knowledge Organization, in *Handbook of Knowledge Management*, Holsapple, C.W. (ed.), Vol. 1, pp. 5–20. Netherlands: Springer Science & Business Media.

Benson, M.L. and Simpson, S.S. (2009). *White-Collar Crime: An Opportunity Perspective, Criminology and Justice Series*. New York: Routledge.

Bergström, O., Hasselbladh, H. and Kärreman, D. (2009). Organizing disciplinary power in knowledge organization, *Scandinavian Journal of Management*, 25, 178–190.

Bjørkelo, B., Ryberg, W., Matthiesen, S.B. and Einarsen, S. (2008). When you talk and talk and nobody listens: A mixed method case study of whistleblowing and its consequences, *International Journal of Organizational Behaviour*, 13 (2), 18–40.

Bock, G.W., Zmud, R.W. and Kim, Y.G. (2005). Behavioral intention formation in knowledge sharing: examining the roles of extrinsic motivators, social-psychological forces, and organizational climate, *MIS Quarterly*, 29 (1), 87–111.

Bonini, S., Court, D. and Marchi, A. (2009). Rebuilding corporate reputations, *McKinsey Quarterly*, 3, 75–83.

Bookman, Z. (2008). Convergences and omissions in reporting corporate and white collar crime, *DePaul Business & Commercial Law Journal*, 6, 347–392.

Brightman, H.J. (2009). *Today's White-Collar Crime: Legal, Investigative, and Theoretical Perspectives*. New York: Routledge.

Brinkmann, J. and Henriksen, A.M. (2008). Vocational ethics as a subspecialty of business ethics — structuring a research and teaching field, *Journal of Business Ethics*, 81, 623–634.

Brody, R.G. and Kiehl, K.A. (2010). From white-collar crime to red-collar crime, *Journal of Financial Crime*, 17 (3), 351–364.

Brody, R.G. and Luo, R. (2009). Fraud and white-collar crime: a Chinese perspective, *Cross Cultural Management*, 16 (3), 317–326.

Brown, J.S. and Duguid, P. (2001). Knowledge and organization: a social-practice perspective, *Organization Science*, 12 (2), 198–213.

Brown, S.D. (2007). The meaning of criminal intelligence. *International Journal of Police Science & Management*, 9 (4), 336–340.

Brown, R., Cannings, A. and Sherriff, J. (2004). Intelligence-led vehicle crime reduction: an evaluation of Operation Gallant, *Home Office Online Report 47/04*, http://www.homeoffice.gov.uk/rds/pdfs04/rdsolr4704.pdf.

Brønn, P.S. and Vidaver-Cohen, D. (2009). Corporate motives for social initiative: legitimacy, sustainability, or the bottom line? *Journal of Business Ethics*, 87, 91–109.

Bucy, P.H., Formby, E.P., Raspanti, M.S. and Rooney, K.E. (2008). Why do they do it?: The motives, mores, and character of white collar criminals, *St. John's Law Review*, 82, 401–571.

Cain, M. (2009). Is crime Giffen? *Journal of Financial Crime*, 16 (1), 80–85.

Capron, L. and Guillén, M. (2009). National corporate governance institutions and post-acquisition target reorganization, *Strategic Management Journal*, 30, 803–830.

Carnegie, G.D. and Napier, C.J. (2010). Traditional accountants and business professionals: Portraying the accounting profession after Enron, *Accounting, Organizations and Society*, 35, 360–376.

Castello, I. and Lozano, J. (2009). From risk management to citizenship corporate social responsibility: analysis of strategic drivers of change, *Corporate Governance*, 9 (4), 373–385.

Chan, S.H., Lowe, D.J. and Yao, L.J. (2008). The legal implications of auditors using a fraud decision aid vs. professional judgment, *Journal of Forensic Accounting*, 9, 63–82.

Cheng, H. and Ma, L. (2009). White collar crime and the criminal justice system — government response to bank fraud and corruption in China, *Journal of Financial Crime*, 16 (2), 166–179.

Chun, R. (2009). A corporate's responsibility to employees during a merger: organizational virtue and employee loyalty, *Corporate Governance*, 9 (4), 473–483.

Collins, J.D., Uhlenbruck, K. and Rodriguez, P. (2009). Why firms engage in corruption: a top management perspective, *Journal of Business Ethics*, 87, 89–108.

Colquitt, J.A. and Zapata-Phelan, C.P. (2007). Trends in theory building and theory testing: a five-decade study of the Academy of Management Journal, *Academy of Management Journal*, 50 (6), 1281–1303.

Corrocher, N., Cusmano, L. and Morrison, A. (2009). Modes of innovation in knowledge-intensive business services evidence from Lombardy, *Journal of Evolutionary Economics*, 19, 173–196.

Council of Europe (2007). Council Conclusions setting the EU priorities for the fight against organized crime based on the 2007 organized crime threat assessment, *Council of the European Union*, Brussels, Belgium.

Courrent, J.M. and Gundolf, K. (2009). Proximity and micro-enterprise manager's ethics: a French empirical study of responsible business attitudes, *Journal of Business Ethics*, 88, 749–762.

Crowson, P. (2009). Adding public value: the limits of corporate responsibility, *Resource Policy*, 34, 105–111.

Crumbley, D.L., Heitger, L.E. and Smith, G.S. (2003). *Forensic and Investigative Accounting*. Chicago, IL: CCH Incorporated.

Crumbley, D.L., Heitger, L.E. and Smith, G.S. (2007). *Forensic and Investigative Accounting*. Chicago, IL: CCH Wolters Kluwer business.

Curtis, G.E. (2008). Legal and regulatory environments and ethics: essential components of a fraud and forensic accounting curriculum, *Issues in Accounting Education*, 23 (4), 535–543.

D'Amato, A. and Roome, N. (2009). Towards an integrated model of leadership for corporate responsibility and sustainable development: a process model of corporate responsibility beyond management innovation, *Corporate Governance*, 9 (4), 421–434.

Demetis, D.S. (2009). Data growth, the new order of information manipulation and consequences for the AML/ATF domains, *Journal of Money Laundering Control*, 12 (4), 353–370.

DiMaggio, P.J. (1995). Comments on 'what theory is not', *Administrative Science Quarterly*, 40, 391–397.

Dion, M. (2008). Ethical leadership and crime prevention in the organizational setting, *Journal of Financial Crime*, 15 (3), 308–319.

Dion, M. (2009). Corporate crime and the dysfunction of value networks, *Journal of Financial Crime*, 16 (4), 436–445.

Dion, M. (2010). Corruption and ethical relativism: what is at stake? *Journal of Financial Crime*, 17 (2), 240–250.

Dowling, G.R. (2006). Communicating corporate reputation through stories, *California Management Review*, 49 (1), 82–100.

EFE (2008). *Årsrapport, Enheten for finansiell etterretning (Annual report, Unit for financial intelligence)*, Økokrim, www.okokrim.no.

EFE (2009). *Årsrapport, Enheten for finansiell etterretning (Annual report, Unit for financial intelligence)*, Økokrim, www.okokrim.no.

Eicher, S. (2009). Government for Hire, in *Corruption in International Business — The Challenge of Cultural and Legal Diversity*, Corporate Social Responsibility Series, Gower Applied Business Research. Farnham, England: Ashgate Publishing Limited.

Einwiller, S.A., Carroll, C.E. and Korn, K. (2010). Under what conditions do the news media influence corporate reputation? the roles of media dependency and need for orientation, *Corporate Reputation Review*, 12 (4), 299–315.

Elvins, M. (2003). Europe's response to transnational organised crime, in *Crime: Perspectives on global security*, Edwards, A. and Gill, P. (eds.), pp. 29–41. London: Routledge.

FATF (2004). *FATF 40 Recommendations*, Financial Action Task Force, www.fatf-gafi.org/dataoecd/7/40/34849567.PDF.

Fichman, R.G. and Kemerer, C.F. (1997). The assimilation of software process innovations: an organizational learning perspective *Management Science*, 43 (10), 1345–1363.

Fijnaut, C. and Huberts, L. (2002). Corruption, Integrity and Law Enforcement, in *Corruption, Integrity and Law Enforcement*, Fijnaut, C. and Huberts, L. (eds.), pp. 3–34. The Hague, The Netherlands: Kluwer Law International.

Frankfort-Nachmias, C. and Nachmias, D. (2002). *Research Methods in the Social Sciences*, 5th Ed. London, UK: Arnold.

Freeman, R.E. and Phillips, R.A. (2002). Stakeholder theory: a libertarian defense. *Business Ethics Quarterly*, 12 (3), 331–349.

Friedman, B.A. (2009). Human resource management role implications for corporate reputation, *Corporate Reputation Review*, 12 (3), 229–244.

Füss, R. and Hecker, A. (2008). Profiling white-collar crime: evidence from German-speaking countries, *Corporate Ownership & Control*, 5 (4), 149–161.

Gabel, J.T.A., Mansfield, N.R. and Houghton, S.M. (2009). Letter vs. spirit: the evolution of compliance into ethics, *American Business Law Journal*, 46 (3), 453–486.

Gallouj, F. and Savona, M. (2009). Innovation in services: a review of the debate and a research agenda, *Journal of Evolutionary Economics*, 19, 149–172.

Garoupa, N. (2007). Optimal law enforcement and criminal organization, *Journal of Economic Behavior & Organization*, 63, 461–474.

Garud, R. and Kumaraswamy, A. (2005). Vicious and virtuous circles in the management of knowledge: the case of Infosys Technologies, *MIS Quarterly*, 29 (1), 9–33.

Godfrey, P.C., Merill, C.B. and Hansen, J.M. (2009). The relationship between corporate social responsibility and shareholder value: an empirical test of the risk management hypothesis, *Strategic Management Journal*, 30, 425–445.

Goldschmidt, L. (2004). The role of boards in preventing economic crime, *Journal of Financial Crime*, 11 (4), 342–346.

Hair, J.F., Black, W.C., Babin, B.J. and Anderson, R.E. (2010). *Multivariate Data Analysis*, 7th Ed. Pearson Education, NJ: Upper Saddle River.

Hall, M. (2010). Accounting information and managerial work, *Accounting, Organizations and Society*, 35, 301–315.

Hammann, E.M., Habisch, A. and Pechlaner, H. (2009). Values that create value: socially responsible business practices in SMEs — empirical evidence from German companies, *Business Ethics: A European Review*, 18 (1), 37–51.

Hansen, L.L. (2009). Corporate financial crime: social diagnosis and treatment, *Journal of Financial Crime*, 16 (1), 28–40.

Harfield, C. (2008). Paradigms, pathologies, and practicalities — policing organized crime in England and Wales, *Policing*, 2 (1), 63–73.

Harreld, J.B., O'Reilly, C.A. and Tushman, M.L. (2007). Dynamic capabilities at IBM: driving strategy into action, *California Management Review*, 49 (4), 21–43.

He, P. (2010). A typological study on money laundering, *Journal of Money Laundering Control*, 13 (1), 15–32.

Heath, J. (2008). Business ethics and moral motivation: a criminological perspective, *Journal of Business Ethics*, 83, 595–614.

Hemphill, T.A. (2006). Corporate internal investigations: balancing firm social reputation with board fiduciary responsibility, *Corporate Governance*, 6 (5), 635–642.

Hemphill, T.A. and Cullari, F. (2009). Corporate governance practices: a proposed policy incentive regime to facilitate internal investigations and self-reporting of criminal activities, *Journal of Business Ethics*, 87, 333–351.

Henning, J. (2009). Perspectives on financial crimes in Roman-Dutch law: bribery, fraud and the general crime of falsity, *Journal of Financial Crime*, 16 (4), 295–304.

Highhouse, S., Brooks, M.E. and Gregarus, G. (2009). An organizational impression management perspective on the formation of corporate reputations, *Journal of Management*, 35 (6), 1481–1493.

Hipp, C. (1999). Knowledge-intensive business services in the new mode of knowledge production, *AI & Society*, 13, 88–106.

Ho, D. and Wong, B. (2008). Issues on compliance and ethics in taxation: what do we know? *Journal of Financial Crime*, 15 (4), 369–382.

Huefner, R.J. (2010). The Forensic Audit: An Example from the Public Sector, *Journal of Forensic & Investigative Accounting*, 2 (1), 1–16, www.bus.lsu.edu/accounting/faculty/lcrumbley/jfia/Articles.htm.

Hughes, K.E., Louwers, T.J. and Reynolds, J.K. (2008). Toward an expanded control environment framework, *Journal of Forensic Accounting*, 9, 115–128.

Ilter, C. (2009). Fraudulent money transfers: a case from Turkey, *Journal of Financial Crime*, 16 (2), 125–136.

Innes, M. and Sheptycki, J.W.E. (2004). From detection to disruption: intelligence and the changing logic of police crime control in the United Kingdom, *International Criminal Justice Review*, 14, 1–24.

Jacopin, T. and Fontrodona, J. (2009). Questioning the corporate responsibility department alignment with the business model of the company, *Corporate Governance*, 9 (4), 528–536.

James, K.L. and Seipel, S.J. (2010). The Effects of Decreased User Confidence on Perceived Internal Audit Fraud Protection, *Journal of Forensic & Investigative Accounting*, 2 (1), 1–23, www.bus.lsu.edu/accounting/faculty/lcrumbley/jfia/Articles.htm.

Jaschke, H.G., Bjørgo, T., Romero, F.del B., Kwanten, C., Mawby, R. and Pogan, M. (2007). *Perspectives of Police Science in Europe*, Final Report, European Police College, CEPOL, Collège Européen de Police, Hampshire, UK.

Jayasuriya, D. (2006). Auditors in a changing regulatory environment, *Journal of Financial Crime*, 13 (1), 51–55.

Johnson, R.A. (2005). Whistleblowing and the police, *Rutgers University Journal of Law and Urban Policy*, 1 (3), 74–83.

Johnson, R.R. (2008). Officer firearms assaults at domestic violence calls: a descriptive analysis, *The Police Journal*, 81 (1), 25–45.

Jones, M. (2009). Governance, integrity, and the police organization, *Policing: An International Journal of Police Strategies & Management*, 32 (2), 338–350.

Joyce, E. (2005). Expanding the International Regime on Money Laundering in Response to Transnational Organized Crime, Terrorism, and Corruption, in *Handbook of Transnational Crime and Justice*, Reichel, P. (ed.), pp. 79–97. London: Sage Publications.

Kark, R. and Dijk, D. van (2007). Motivation to lead, motivation to follow: the role of the self-regulatory focus in leadership processes, *Academy of Management Review*, 32 (2), 500–528.

Kazanjian, R.K. and Drazin, R. (1989). An empirical test of a stage of growth progression model, *Management Science*, 35 (12), 1489–1503.

Keh, H.T. and Xie, Y. (2009). Corporate reputation and customer behavioral intentions: the roles of trust, identification and commitment, *Industrial Marketing Management*, 38, 732–742.

Kempa, M. (2010). Combating white-collar crime in Canada: serving victim needs and market integrity, *Journal of Financial Crime*, 17 (2), 251–264.

King, W.R. and Teo, T.S.H. (1997). Integration between business planning and information systems planning: validating a stage hypothesis. *Decision Science*, 28 (2), 279–308.

Kranacher, M.J., Morris, B.W., Pearson, T.A. and Riley, A. (2008). A model curriculum for education in fraud and forensic accounting, *Issues in Accounting Education*, 23 (4), 505–519.

Laise, D., Migliarese, P. and Venteremo, S. (2005). Knowledge organisation design: a diagnostic tool. *Human Systems Management*, 24, 121–131.

Lange, D. (2008). A multidimensional conceptualization of organizational corruption control, *The Academy of Management Review*, 33 (3), 710–729.

Langfield-Smith, K. and Smith, D. (2003). Management control systems and trust in outsourcing relationships, *Management Accounting Research*, 14 (3), 281–307.

Lassen, C., Laugen, B.T. and Næss, P. (2006). Virtual mobility and organizational reality — a note on the mobility needs in knowledge organizations, *Transportation Research*, Part D, 11, 459–463.

Laudon, K.C. and Laudon, J.P. (2010). *Management Information Systems: Managing the Digital Firm*, 11th Ed. London, UK: Pearson Education.

Lee, C.C. and Welker, R.B. (2010). Does familiarity with an interviewee's white lying make it easier to detect the interviewee's deceptions? *Journal of Forensic & Investigative Accounting*, 2 (1), 1–36, www.bus.lsu.edu/accounting/faculty/lcrumbley/jfia/Articles.htm.

Leonard-Barton, D. (1992). Core capabilities and core rigidities: a paradox in managing product development, *Strategic Management Journal*, 13, 111–125.

Liebowitz, J. (2004). Will knowledge management work in the government? *Electronic Government: An International Journal*, 1 (1), 1–7.

Linthicum, C., Reitenga, A.L. and Sanchez, J.M. (2010). Social responsibility and corporate reputation: the case of the Arthur Andersen Enron audit failure, *Journal of Accounting and Public Policy*, 29, 160–176.

Liu, C.C. and Chen, S.Y. (2005). Determinants of knowledge sharing of e-learners, *International Journal of Innovation and Learning*, 2 (4), 434–445.

Love, E.G. and Kraatz, M. (2009). Character, conformity, or the bottom line? How and why downsizing affected corporate reputation, *Academy of Management Journal*, 52 (2), 314–335.

Maak, T. (2008). Undivided corporate responsibility: towards a theory of corporate integrity, *Journal of Business Ethics*, 82, 353–368.

Madhavaram, S. and Hunt, S.D. (2008). The service-dominant logic and a hierarchy of operant resources: developing masterful operant resources and implications for marketing strategy, *Journal of the Academy of Marketing Science*, 36, 67–82.

Maghan, J. (1994). Intelligence gathering approaches in prisons, *Low Intensity Conflict & Law Enforcement*, 3 (3), 548–557.

Markovski, S. and Hall, P. (2007). Public sector entrepreneurship and the production of defence, *Public Finance and Management*, 7 (3), 260–294.

Matten, D. and Moon, J. (2008). "Implicit" and "explicit" CSR: a conceptual framework for a comparative understanding of corporate social responsibility, *Academy of Management Review*, 33 (2), 404–424.

Miri-Lavassani, K., Kumar, V., Movahedi, B. and Kumar, U. (2009). Developing an identity measurement model: a factor analysis approach, *Journal of Financial Crime*, 16 (4), 364–386.

Misangyi, V.F., Weaver, G.R. and Elms, H. (2008). Ending corruption: the interplay among institutional logics, resources, and institutional entrepreneurs, *The Academy of Management Review*, 33 (3), 750–798.

Moore, G., Slack, R. and Gibbon, J. (2009). Criteria for responsible business practice in SMEs: an exploratory case of U.K. fair trade organizations, *Journal of Business Ethics*, 89, 173–188.

Mostovicz, I., Kakabadse, N. and Kakabadse, A. (2009). CSR: the role of leadership in driving ethical outcomes, *Corporate Governance*, 9 (4), 448–460.

Nambisan, S. (2002) Designing virtual customer environments for new product development: toward a theory, *Academy of Management Review*, 27 (3), 392–413.

Nestor, S. (2004). The impact of changing corporate governance norms on economic crime, *Journal of Financial Crime*, 11 (4), 347–352.

Neumann, B.R., Crowdes, M. and Neumann, D. (2010). A Forensic Audit of Staffing and Census in a Long-Term Care Facility, *Journal of Forensic & Investigative Accounting*, 2 (1), 1–28, www.bus.lsu.edu/accounting/faculty/lcrumbley/jfia/Articles.htm.

Neuser, D.J. (2005). How to conduct effective internal investigations of workplace matters, *Employee Relations Law Journal*, 31 (1), 67–89.

Nolan, J. and Taylor, L. (2009). Corporate responsibility for economic, social and cultural rights: rights in search of a remedy? *Journal of Business Ethics*, 87, 433–451.

Nolan, R.L. (1979). Managing the crisis in data processing, *Harvard Business Review*, 57 (2), 115–126.

Nonaka, I., Toyama, R. and Konno, N. (2000). SECI, Ba and leadership: a unified model of dynamic knowledge creation. *Long Range Planning*, 33 (1), 5–34.

Norman, C.S., Rose, A.M. and Rose, J.M. (2010). Internal audit reporting lines, fraud risk decomposition, and assessments of fraud risk, *Accounting, Organizations and Society*, 36, 1–10.

Nunnally, J.C. and Bernstein, I.H. (1994). *Psychometric Theory*, 3rd Ed. New York, NY: McGraw-Hill.

O'Connor, T.R. (2005). Police Deviance and Ethics. http://www.policecrimes.com/police-deviance.html.

Omoyele, O. (2008). Corporate governance as a contraption of the FSA's accountability — an exegesis of the combined code, *Journal of Financial Crime*, 15 (19), 82–103.

OPI (2007). Report on the 'Kit Walker' Investigations, office of Police Integrity, Melbourne, Victoria, Australia, www.opi.vic.gov.au [1 September 2010].

Pearson, T.C. (2010). Enron's banks escape liability: Reconsidering the accounting profession's opposition to private party litigation to prevent third-parties from assisting in fraud, *Journal of Forensic & Investigative Accounting*, 2 (1), 1–22, www.bus.lsu.edu/accounting/faculty/lcrumbley/jfia/Articles.htm.

Pfarrer, M.D., DeCelles, K.A., Smith, K.G. and Taylor, M.S. (2008). After the fall: reintegrating the corrupt organization, *The Academy of Management Review*, 33 (3), 730–749.

Pickett, K.H.S. and Picket, J.M. (2002). *Financial Crime Investigation and Control*. New York: John Wiley & Sons.

Pierce, J.L., Kostova, T. and Dirks, K.T. (2001) Toward a theory of psychological ownership in organizations, *Academy of Management Review*, 6 (2), 298–310.

Ping, H. (2005). The suspicious transactions reporting system, *Journal of Money Laundering Control*, 8 (3), 252–259.

Pinto, J., Leana, C.R. and Pil, F.K. (2008). Corrupt organizations or organizations of corrupt individuals? Two types of organization-level corruption, *The Academy of Management Review*, 33 (3), 685–709.

Porter, L.E. and Warrender, C. (2009). A multivariate model of police deviance: examining the nature of corruption, crime and misconduct, *Policing & Society*, 19 (1), 79–99.

Poston, R.S. and Speier, C. (2005). Effective use of knowledge management systems: a process model of content ratings and credibility indicators. *MIS Quarterly*, 29 (2), 221–244.

Prahalad, C.K. and Hamel, G. (1990). The core competence of the corporation, *Harvard Business Review*, 76 (3), 79–91.

Prenzler, T. (2009). *Police Corruption: Preventing Misconduct and Maintaining Integrity*. Boca Raton, FL: CRC Press, Taylor & Francis Group.

Punch, M. (2003). Rotten orchards: pestilence, police misconduct and system failure, *Policing and Society*, 13, (2) 171–196.

PwC (2007). *Economic Crime: People, Culture and Controls*, 4th Biennial Global Economic Crime Survey, PricewaterhouseCoopers.

Quarantelli, E.L. (2008). Conventional beliefs and counterintuitive realities, *Social Research*, 75 (3), 873–904.

Quinn, J.B. (1999). Strategic outsourcing: leveraging knowledge capabilities, *Sloan Management Review*, Summer, 9–21.

Ramamoorti, S. (2008). The psychology and sociology of fraud: integrating the behavioral sciences component into fraud and forensic accounting curricula, *Issues in Accounting Education*, 23 (4), 521–533.

Ratcliffe, J.H. (2008). *Intelligence-Led Policing*. Devon, UK: Willan Publishing.

Riffe, D. and Freitag, A. (1997). A content analysis of content analyses, twenty-five years of journalism quarterly, *Journalism Mass Communication Quarterly*, 74, 873–882.

Robson, R.A. (2010). Crime and punishment: rehabilitating retribution as a justification for organizational criminal liability, *American Business Law Journal*, 47 (1), 109–144.

Rok, B. (2009). Ethical context of the participative leadership model: taking people into account, *Corporate Governance*, 9 (4), 461–472.

Rothwell, G.R. and Baldwin, J.N. (2006). Ethical climates and contextual predictors of whistle-blowing, *Review of Public Personnel Administration*, 26 (3), 216–244.

Rothwell, G.R. and Baldwin, J.N. (2007). Whistle-blowing and the code of silence in police agencies, *Crime and Delinquency*, 53 (4), 605–632.

Schneider, S. (2004). Organized crime, money laundering, and the real estate market in Canada, *Journal of Property Research*, 21 (2), 99–118.

Shankman, N.A. (1999). Reframing the debate between agency and stakeholder theories of the firm. *Journal of Business Ethics*, 19 (4), 319–334.

Sheehan, N.T. and Stabell, C.B. (2007). Discovering new business models for knowledge intensive organizations, *Strategy & Leadership*, 35 (2), 22–29.

Sheptycki, J. (2007). Police ethnography in the house of serious and organized crime, in *Transformations of Policing*, Henry, A. and Smith, D.J. (eds), pp. 51–77. Oxford, UK: Ashgate Publishing.

Skousen, C.J. and Wright, C.J. (2008). Contemporaneous risk factors and the prediction of financial statement fraud, *Journal of Forensic Accounting*, 9, 37–62.

Smith, H.L. (2003). Knowledge organization and local economic development: the cases of Oxford and Grenoble, *Regional Studies*, 37 (9), 899–909.

Spitzeck, H. (2009). The development of governance structures for corporate responsibility, *Corporate Governance*, 9 (4), 495–505.

Stansbury, J.M. and Victor, B. (2009). Whistle-blowing among young employees: a life-course perspective, *Journal of Business Ethics*, 85, 281–299.

Stedje, S. (2004). *The Man in the Street, or the Man in the Suite: An Evaluation of the Effectiveness in the Detection of Money Laundering in Norway*, MA Social Sciences and Law Criminal Intelligence Analysis/CIA, The University of Manchester, UK.

Sutton, R.I. and Staw, B.M. (1995). What theory is not, *Administrative Science Quarterly*, 40, 371–384.

SYPIS (2007). *South Yorkshire Police Intelligence Strategy 2007 — Breaking the chain*, South Yorkshire Police, UK.

Søreide, T. (2006). *Business corruption: Incidence, mechanisms, and consequences*, thesis submitted for the degree of Dr. Oecon at the Norwegian School of Economics and Business Administration, Bergen, Norway.

Taylor, A. and Greve, H.R. (2006). Superman or the fantastic four? Knowledge combination and experience in innovative teams, *Academy of Management Journal*, 49 (4), 723–740.

Tellechea, A.F. (2008). Economic crimes in the capital markets, *Journal of Financial Crime*, 15 (2), 214–222.

Thomas, A. and Mancino, A. (2007). The relationship between entrepreneurial characteristics, firms' positioning and local development, *Entrepreneurship and Innovation*, 8 (2), 105–114.

Toner, G.A. (2009). New ways of thinking about old crimes: prosecuting corruption and organized criminal groups engaged in labour-management racketeering, *Journal of Financial Crime*, 16 (1), 41–59.

Tong, S. (2007). *Training the Effective Detective: Report of Recommendations*, University of Cambridge, Canterbury Christ Church University, Kent, UK.

Trochim, W.M. (2006). Research Methods Knowledge Base, http://www. socialresearchmethods.net/kb.

Turner, K.L. and Makhija, M.V. (2006). The role of organizational controls in managing knowledge, *Academy of Management Review*, 31 (1), 197–217.

UNODC (2006). *The Integrity and Accountability of the Police: Criminal justice assessment toolkit*, United Nations Office of Drugs and Crime (UNODC), Vienna International Center, Vienna, Austria, www.unodc.org.

Uretsky, M. (2001). Preparing for the real knowledge organization, *Journal of Organizational Excellence*, 21 (1), 87–93.

Vadera, A.K., Aguilera, R.V. and Caza, B.B. (2009). Making sense of whistle-blowing's antecedents: learning from research on identity and ethics programs, *Business Ethics Quarterly*, 19 (4), 553–586.

Varelius, J. (2009). Is whistle-blowing compatible with employee loyalty? *Journal of Business Ethics*, 85, 263–275.

Venkatesh, V. (2000). Determinants of perceived ease of use: integrating control, intrinsic motivation, and emotion into technology acceptance model, *Information Systems Research*, 11 (4), 342–365.

Venkatesh, V. and Davis, F.D. (2000). A theoretical extension of the technology acceptance model: four longitudinal field studies, *Management Science*, 46 (2), 186–204.

Ventura, M. and Daniel, S.J. (2010). Opportunities for fraud and embezzlement in religious organizations: An exploratory study, *Journal of Forensic & Investigative Accounting*, 2 (1), 1–35, www.bus.lsu.edu/accounting/faculty/lcrumbley/jfia/Articles.htm.

Waddock, S. and McIntosh, M. (2009). Beyond corporate responsibility: implications for management development, *Business and Society Review*, 114 (3), 295–325.

Walker, K. (2010). A systematic review of the corporate reputation literature: definition, measurement, and theory, *Corporate Reputation Review*, 12 (4), 357–387.

Wasko, M.M. and Faraj, S. (2005). Why should I share? Examining social capital and knowledge contribution in electronic networks of practice, *MIS Quarterly*, 29 (1), 35–57.

Weick, K.E. (1995). What theory is not, theorizing is, *Administrative Science Quarterly*, 40, 385–390.

Weismann, M.F. (2009). The foreign corrupt practices act: the failure of the self-regulatory model of corporate governance in the global business environment, *Journal of Business Ethics*, 88, 615–661.

Wettstein, F. (2010). For better or for worse: corporate responsibility beyond "do no harm", *Business Ethics Quarterly*, 20 (2), 275–283.

Wilburn, K. (2009). A model for partnering with not-for-profits to develop socially responsible businesses in a global environment, *Journal of Business Ethics*, 85, 111–120.

Wilhelmsen, S. (2009). *Maximising Organizational Information Sharing and Effective Intelligence Analysis in Critical Data Sets*, Dissertation for the degree of philosophiae doctor (PhD), University of Bergen, Norway.

Williams, J.W. (2008). Out of place and out of line: positioning the police in the regulation of financial markets, *Law & Policy*, 30 (3), 306–335.

Williams, S. and Williams, N. (2003). The business value of business intelligence, *Business Intelligence Journal*, Fall, 30–39.

Zahra, S.A., Kuratko, D.F. and Jennings, D.F. (1999). Entrepreneurship and the acquisition of dynamic organizational capabilities, *Entrepreneurship Theory and Practice*, Spring, 5–10.

Zander, I. (2007). Do you see what I mean? An entrepreneurship perspective on the nature and boundaries of the firm, *Journal of Management Studies*, 44 (7), 1141–1164.

Zheng, W., Yang, B. and McLean, G.N. (2010). Linking organizational culture, structure, strategy, and organizational effectiveness: mediating role of knowledge management, *Journal of Business Research*, 63, 763–771.

Zollo, M., Minoja, M., Casanova, L., Hockerts, K., Neergaard, P., Schneider, S. and Tencati, A. (2009). Towards an internal change management perspective of CSR: evidence from project RESPONSE on the sources of cognitive alignment between managers and their stakeholders, and their implications for social performance, *Corporate Governance*, 9 (4), 355–372.

Økokrim (2008). *Annual Report 2007*, Norwegian National Authority for Investigation and Prosecution of Economic and Environmental Crime, Oslo, Norway.

Index

accountability, 10, 57, 66, 80, 87, 88, 91, 92, 111, 117, 156
accountant role, 123
accounting data, 68, 119
accounting scandal, 117
activity organization, 147
algorithm, 132, 133
analyzing, 20, 60, 142, 151, 157, 163, 166
antisocial behavior, 45
Arthur Andersen, 1, 2, 29, 36, 37, 41, 119

bank depositing, 128
bankruptcy, 68, 117–120, 166
board of directors, 45, 64
business community, 31
business corruption, 15

cash smuggling, 128
CEO, 22, 40, 56, 57, 67, 88, 90, 111
citizenship rights, 67
civil litigation, 55, 56
code of silence, 72, 73
collective panic, 45
communities of practice, 141
comparative analysis, 124, 125
competitive advantage, 30, 31, 34, 136, 137, 146, 153, 154, 162
competitive environment, 159
complexity, 15, 20, 21, 24, 25, 99, 131–133, 137, 140
compliance planing, 63
compliance process, 65

compliance violation, 65
computer, 5, 117, 119, 130–132, 149, 150, 152, 167
computer forensics, 117
computer system, 130–132
confronting, 50, 51, 159
conscious communication, 59
content analysis, 23, 41, 50, 91
control authorities, 169, 170
controlling, 59, 63, 92, 93, 143, 151
core competence, 153, 154
corporate crime, 5, 7, 10–12, 14, 25, 48, 68, 82, 168
corporate entity, 44
corporate environment, 63
corporate initiatives, 95
corporate investigation, 53, 55, 169
corporate personality, 11
corporate self-restraint, 69
corporate worth, 31
corporation, 1, 10–12, 15, 16, 21, 25, 27–29, 33–35, 44, 45, 50, 56, 63, 65–68, 75, 80, 81, 86, 88, 90, 95, 96, 105–109, 114, 122, 181
crime notification, 165
crime scandal, 39
criminal investigation, 55, 56, 177
criminal record, 6, 165
cultural rights, 63
customer satisfaction, 30, 46
customer trust, 33, 46

data mart, 142, 143
data storage, 169, 170

data warehouse, 142, 143
deception detection, 122–124
decision making, 47, 48, 57, 68, 69, 82, 88, 106, 138, 142, 143, 151, 164, 179
detective effectiveness, 59
detective skills, 58, 60
dynamic capabilities, 155, 158–160, 162

economic crime, 18, 81, 82
effective competition, 155
embezzlement, 3–5, 17, 19, 126, 128
employee attraction, 30, 33, 46
employee loyalty, 70, 71, 75, 112
Enron, 1, 2, 4, 11, 25, 29, 36, 37, 39, 41, 42, 68, 69, 80, 117, 119, 120
entrepreneur, 103, 156–158
entrepreneurial culture, 157
ethical behavior, 36, 69
ethics, 47, 48, 50, 54, 64, 66, 67, 70, 71, 86, 90–94, 111
external auditor, 50, 57, 63, 67, 71, 82, 83, 91, 109, 112, 121, 155

financial authorities, 55
financial crime, 2, 3, 6, 7, 9, 11, 18, 23, 71, 85, 86, 108, 117, 119, 126, 127, 165, 166, 169, 171, 173–176, 178
financial restatement, 37
financial scandal, 25, 68
financial statement, 37, 45, 68, 79, 119, 124, 125
financial status, 45
forensic accounting, 2, 55, 68, 117–120, 123, 124, 166, 171
fraud theory, 19

generic knowledge, 60
Glitnir Bank, 69
global business, 69
governance rating, 37

horizontal analysis, 124

impression management, 31, 33
improper payments, 65
influencing, 63, 79, 92, 93

information source, 123, 165–171, 174
innovation, 100, 114, 139–141, 152, 153, 155, 157, 160–162
insider trading, 3–5, 17, 81, 128
institutional theory, 33
insurance claiming, 128
intangible resource, 30, 31, 45
integrity, 21, 57, 60, 64, 66, 67, 89–91, 98, 107, 111
integrity violation, 57
intelligence work, 145, 165
intelligence-led policing, 163, 164
internal control, 23, 50, 63, 66, 91, 92, 94, 117
internal investigation, 2, 49, 51, 53, 54, 165
internal procedures, 64, 91
internet, 5, 167, 168, 170
interview, 37, 54, 55, 58, 61, 123, 166, 170, 171
investigating, 49–51, 53, 165–167, 171, 173, 175, 179
investigation implementation, 177, 179
investigative knowledge, 119, 171, 174, 175
investment performance, 131

judicial court, 73

knowledge production, 141, 161

leadership, 36, 45, 47–49, 67, 80, 88, 89, 91, 92, 95, 101, 110, 111, 138, 148, 159, 160, 171
learning organization, 139, 148, 152, 153
legal knowledge, 60, 145, 172, 174, 175
life-course model, 70
logical sequence, 177

mental health, 45
morality, 35, 47, 48, 108, 120

objective model, 129
occupational crime, 7, 10–14
organizational ability, 141

organizational culture, 9, 41, 42, 47, 72, 107, 135, 148
organizational intelligence, 139

performance evaluation, 179
personal belief, 145
police investigation, 123, 139, 144
practical knowledge, 60
problem organization, 147
procedural knowledge, 136, 145, 172
provocation, 167, 170
public interest, 57, 70, 72, 73
public relations, 32, 35, 83, 85

ratio analysis, 125
regulatory scrutiny, 55, 57
reporting, 18, 19, 49, 50, 55, 64–67, 73, 79, 80, 95, 118, 120, 125, 126, 129, 130, 142, 143, 165, 166
reputation survey, 39, 41
resource management, 32, 43, 59, 161
resource-based theory, 29, 30, 32–34, 44, 153, 158
restatement firm, 37
retaliation, 73–75
risk areas, 65
role abandonment, 45
rotten apple, 13, 14, 88
routine training, 66

self-presentation theory, 34
self-regulatory model, 69
service, 2, 27, 30, 37, 42, 67, 69, 74, 88, 118, 122, 139, 143, 145, 146, 149, 153, 154, 156, 158, 160–162, 166

Siemens, 2, 4, 39, 69
signaling theory, 33, 34
social influence, 66, 100
socially responsible, 49, 67, 94, 95
solution choice, 179
Sponsor Service, 2, 42, 69
stakeholder, 1, 16, 27–35, 44, 45, 47, 70, 79–81, 86, 95, 97, 105, 106, 109, 111, 139
strategic insight, 159
strategic orientation, 157
strategic significance, 155
subjective model, 129, 130
substantive attributes, 31
surveillance, 10, 159, 165, 167, 168, 170
suspicious transactions, 2, 50, 125, 126, 129–133, 169
symbolic attributes, 31
systemic interference, 133

theory of embezzlement, 19
transparency, 35, 47, 64, 65, 80, 95, 148, 168

utility theory, 19

valuation studies, 68, 119
value organization, 148
variance analysis, 124, 125
vertical analysis, 124, 125

whistle blower, 71–75
witness report, 165
work process, 145, 171, 176
WorldCom, 2, 25, 39, 68, 69, 120